PERCEPTION, CONSCIOUSNESS, MEMORY
Reflections of a Biologist

PERCEPTION, CONSCIOUSNESS, MEMORY

Reflections of a Biologist

G. ÁDÁM

Member of the Hungarian Academy of Sciences
Professor of Physiology
Eötvös Loránd University, Budapest, Hungary

PLENUM PRESS · NEW YORK AND LONDON

Translated by
K. TAKÁCSI-NAGY

Published in the U.S.A. by
PLENUM PRESS

a division of
PLENUM PUBLISHING CORPORATION
227 West 17th Street, New York, N.Y. 10011

Library of Congress Catalog Card Number 73-20153
ISBN 0-306-30776-6

Joint edition published with
AKADÉMIAI KIADÓ, BUDAPEST, HUNGARY

Contents

PART II

THE ENERGETICS OF MENTAL PROCESSES:
THE WAKING STATE, SLEEP, ATTENTION,
AND CONSCIOUSNESS

Chapter 7

Preface

The interdisciplinary approach so popular today is more than a matter of fashion. It is, in fact, a reflection of the recognition that a good many areas once considered adequately treated by one or the other of the traditional disciplines straddle the boundaries of several.

Interdisciplinary research then is, by definition, a cooperative venture by several autonomous branches of science into areas incompletely accessible to any one of them. By stimulating cooperation among several related disciplines, such research may serve to enrich each of them; but, on the other hand, the existence of these border areas occasionally serves as a pretext for postponing the solution of seemingly insurmountable problems.

Brain research seems to have become such a border area of science. The fortress of classical psychology is being assaulted before our very eyes, its peripheral and even its more integral areas being invaded by physiology, morphology, physics, and chemistry. Neurophysiology, too, has ceased to be an autonomous and self-governing field, and has come increasingly to rely on the help proffered by general psychology, epistemology, and logic, as well as exact sciences such as mathematics and physics. These border assaults have undoubtedly been beneficial for all involved.

Within the traditional boundaries of their stuffy principles most classical disciplines are today facing a methodological and epistemological crisis. The breaching of their walls may at least hold out some hope of a renaissance.

The author of this book is active in the field of neurophysiology. Along with several of his colleagues he expects progress to be most rapid in the border areas of this discipline, and believes in throwing the doors of brain research wide open to psychologists, mathematicians, philosophers, physicists, engineers, and the medical profession. However, communication among those working in different fields is impeded by the lack of a common language even within the natural sciences, let alone the arts. A neurophysiologist cannot, therefore, but use the terminology of his own field and hope that those who might be interested in this book have acquired sufficient experience in exploring unknown paths.

Interest in the working of the human brain is growing in all walks of scientific life. In this country, but elsewhere, too, a great number of physicists, mathematicians, electrical engineers, and philosophers are concerned with different aspects of the functioning of the nervous system. It is a sign of this interest that the author has repeatedly been invited by different university departments outside his own field to lecture on brain physiology.

The present book was written with the interest of the audiences of these lectures in mind: the philosopher and teacher who needed to know more about the biology of cerebral reflection and of storing mechanisms to be able to go on with his work; and the physicist and electrical engineer who wished to apply his up-to-date knowledge of information theory or communications to brain research. Even the older generation of biologists, doctors, and psychologists interested in the recent results of brain research might welcome a concise and "easily digestible" summary of this kind to brush up their knowledge of neuro-physiology.

In this sense, this is a popular scientific book. Apart from the author's own research, it has been based on the most important work on brain physiology published in recent years; but outstanding popular scientific periodicals have also been consulted, especially in the selection of the illustrations.

The first Hungarian edition was received with interest and was quickly sold out. One might attribute this to its having been published at a time when the results of brain research accumulated at an amazing rate. This English edition, which closely follows a second Hungarian and a German edition, is a sign of unflagging interest.

The subject matter discussed has been limited to the biological processes of cerebral information uptake, processing, and storage. The choice has not been prompted solely by the author's own research interests, but by the conviction that sensory "afferent" processes represent the group of higher nervous mechanisms that most nearly approximate the interests of other disciplines.

This book was also written for the layman; if it succeeds in arousing popular interest in brain physiology the author will consider his time well spent.

G. Ádám

Part I

Perception—information uptake of the mind

The old adage *"Nihil in intellectu, quod non ante in sensu"* "Nothing may take place in the mind that has not been in the senses," though such an oversimplification is hardly tenable today, is still felt to contain some truth. Information from the environment can reach the brain, i.e., the center where it is processed, only via the sensory system, which may thus be regarded as the gateway of the mind or, using computer jargon, an information input device.

Our knowledge of the complex mechanisms triggered by environmental stimuli and resulting in subjective sensations is still rather scanty. A number of basic processes have been cleared up, but important connections on a larger scale still await clarification.

We know that the sensory neuron—the receptor—transforms the stimulus into short, rhythmic electrochemical impulses. The train of impulses is then transmitted by nervous pathways to different relay stations of the central nervous system. The mechanism whereby the impulses travel from one neuron to the next is known. Some details of the central "decoding" process have also been elucidated. However, the physiological interpretation of the entire sensory function, or rather a uniform neurophysiological theory of perception that would answer all the problems of the central representation of the senses, is still lacking.

In the following we try to summarize what the biologist's measuring and registering devices reveal about the peripheral receptors and their cerebral representations.

Chapter 1

The biology of perception

Like the physiologist concerned with theoretical prob- **The analyzer**
lems, the clinician dealing with the pathology of sense organs is no longer able to separate the function of the receptor apparatus from its cerebral representation. Sensory
information is received, transmitted, and processed by a
functional unit which consists of *receptors* (e.g., the retina
or the organ of Corti in the inner ear), *sensory nerve pathways*, and *cerebral neurons*. This apparatus has been called
"analyzer" by Pavlov, referring to its stimulus-analyzing
function. Before dealing with the groups of central nerve
cells having a sensory role in the psychological sense, let
us briefly describe the general characteristics of peripheral
receptor function.

Experimental techniques

Micromethods which allow the study of functional
changes within the cell or even in subcellular structures are
increasingly used in the study of the physiology of sense

organs. The methods of microscopic anatomy have long been used to investigate the structure of receptors, which is well known within the limits of the resolving power of the light microscope. The fine structure of the receptor apparatus is now being studied by electron microscopy with the aim of elucidating intricate connections between structure and function.

The future of microphysiology   It is hard to predict of how much use the results of micromorphological studies will be in solving psychological problems. The techniques of microphysiology, on the other hand, have proved a valuable tool in following the nervous impulse generated in the receptors by external stimuli and in measuring its parameters. Tiny electrodes, measurable in microns, are inserted into the receptor cells to record their resting potential and the sudden change in their voltage called action potential.

The classical techniques of receptor physiology are *macromethods* studying the cerebral changes ensuing in response to external stimuli in healthy subjects with intact nervous systems. One group of these methods belong to the realm of *psychophysics*. These are based on the subjective reports of the test subjects following exposure to stimuli of measurable intensity generated by well-known physical sources. *Conditioning* used to establish differentiation between two stimuli also belongs here. The method, which will be discussed in detail later on, consists in associating (reinforcing) one of the stimuli with an unconditioned stimulus (e.g., food). If the animal is able to distinguish between the two stimuli, it will respond to the conditioned (reinforced) stimulus, but not to the other stimulus presented alone.

18

Generation and conduction of impulses

In the course of phylogenesis specialized organs have developed for the reception and transmission of external stimuli. The *receptors* are specialized structures converting external stimuli into electrochemical signals called *impulses* which are then transmitted along the nervous pathway to the sensory cortex. The receptors are in close structural contact with the appropriate nerve cells, more precisely with their processes conducting the impulses generated in the receptors to the cell body (soma). The main function of the nerve cell (neuron) is to transmit the impulses generated in the receptors. Naturally, the function of the individual neurons varies in the animal and human organism: some of them are capable of firing rhythmic impulses, others analyze and integrate the impulses arriving at them. In the present discussion we shall only deal with the role of the neuron as transmitter of impulses. In a simplified form it might be stated that the generation of impulses is the task of the receptor, while their transmission is accomplished by the neurons. Let us see both functions.

To understand the propagation of the short, periodic electrochemical pulses, we must first have a look at the resting state of the neuron. Normally there is a difference in voltage of approximately 30 to 100 mV between the inside and outside of the receptor cell in the resting state. This is what we call the *resting potential*. This difference can be measured by inserting a microelectrode of about 1 μm diameter into the cell and placing another electrode outside the cell membrane. The potential difference can be recorded by a suitably sensitive instrument. The reason for this potential difference is still being debated. One thing is certain, however: the fluid found within the cell, i.e., the intracellular fluid, differs in chemical composition from that found outside, i.e., the extracellular fluid. While within the cell there is an excess of potassium ions, the tissue fluid contains sodium ions in higher numbers. The cell contains much protein (the protoplasm, too, has a protein structure), while outside the cell membrane chlorine ions may be found in great numbers. The presence of potassium and the absence of sodium in the cell is presumably due to what we call the "sodium pump," i.e., active metabolic processes of the cell. The potential difference at rest is sufficiently explained, according to Hodgkin, by the uneven distribution of ions.

Analog process   If the receptor cell is stimulated, the magnitude of the resting potential is reduced by 30–50 mV, and a state of hypopolarization ensues. In this state a second stimulus of much lower intensity is sufficient to cause the resting potential to break down. The lowering of the potential in the receptor cell just mentioned is highly localized, i. e., the reduction in voltage occurs just at the portion of the cell membrane which has been exposed to the stimulus. Another characteristic of the hypopolarized state is that the degree of the potential change depends on the intensity of the stimulus: weaker stimuli lower the resting potential only slightly, while strong stimuli result in a more pronounced hypopolarization. It might also be said that this local voltage reduction is proportional to the external stimulus; that is why, in the terminology of information theory, it can be called an *analog process*.

This local reduction in voltage which has an analog character is called *generator potential* by biophysicists. The generator potential of the receptor is called *receptor potential* by some authors. This local change in voltage is a very important phenomenon, because it gives rise to the generation of nervous impulses in the axon connected with the receptor cell. This impulse does not remain local but is propagated and—as will be seen—is not analog, but—again borrowing the language of computers—digital in character.

20

The receptor potential is frequently studied in the *Paci-* Pacinian corpuscle
nian corpuscle found in great numbers in the skin and other
tissues—and also in the peritoneum—of humans and animals. It is constructed like an onion and responds to pressure, i.e., to mechanical force altering its structure (Fig. 1).
The receptor potential is produced in the nerve ending
embedded in the Pacinian corpuscle, and is subsequently
propagated toward other parts of the neuron in the form
of periodic impulses.

The structure of the neuron is shown in Fig. 2. The body
of the nerve cell is star-shaped or slightly rounded in the
brain and nervous tissue of most animal species. The most
conspicuous feature of the neuron is that is has a number of
root-like processes. The short ramifying fibers are called
dendrites; they generally have a stimulus-receiving function. The long single fiber frequently having a myelin
sheath is called the *axon*. Its function is the conduction of
nervous impulses. While the dendrites may be absent from
some neurons, no nerve cell in any animal species can be
without an axon. The axon (or nerve fiber) is the most important structure in impulse conduction and an integral
part of the nervous pathways.

If hypopolarization in the receptor cell exceeds the Digital process
threshold of the axon of the cell, depolarization of the axon
ensues. This sudden change in voltage is termed *action*
potential. As we have seen, the resting potential was only
reduced in the receptor. In the axon, however, this potential
completely disappears; moreover, for a thousandth of a
second—or even less—the inside of the fiber becomes
slightly positive with respect to the surrounding fluid.

This "reversion" of voltage is *periodically repeated*. At the
moment of the maximum of the action potential (spike)
the axon membrane is refractory to fresh stimuli, and another pulse will arise only after the membrane has recovered
its normal state of polarization. This is how the train of
pulses characterizing nervous conduction takes shape.

21

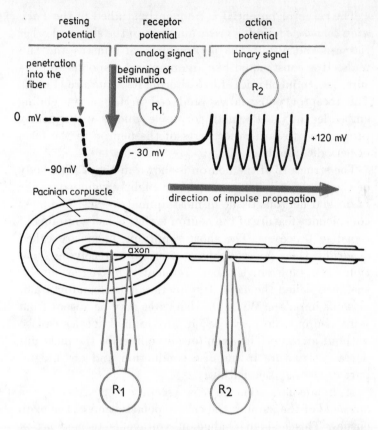

Fig. 1. Generation and propagation of nervous impulse in the Pacinian corpuscle and in the axon embedded in the receptor. R_1 and R_2 denote recordings by microelectrodes. The receptor potential and the periodic action potential are shown at the top.

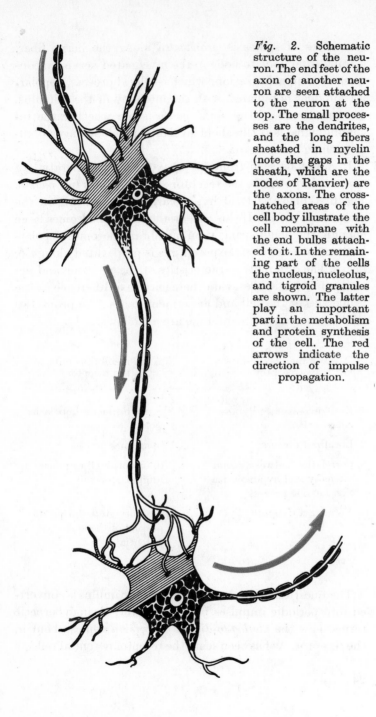

Fig. 2. Schematic structure of the neuron. The end feet of the axon of another neuron are seen attached to the neuron at the top. The small processes are the dendrites, and the long fibers sheathed in myelin (note the gaps in the sheath, which are the nodes of Ranvier) are the axons. The cross-hatched areas of the cell body illustrate the cell membrane with the end bulbs attached to it. In the remaining part of the cells the nucleus, nucleolus, and tigroid granules are shown. The latter play an important part in the metabolism and protein synthesis of the cell. The red arrows indicate the direction of impulse propagation.

The series of spikes is *propagated* along the nerve fiber, leaping from node to node in the myelinated nerve. In contrast to hypopolarization, which is a local process, depolarization does not change with the intensity of the stimulus. The amplitude of the spike is the same whether the incoming signal is at threshold level or is much stronger ("all-or-nothing" response).

Two types of potential: two types of membrane

It might be seen from the above that the generation of nervous impulses in the receptor structures has *two phases*. The first phase is local hypopolarization resulting in the receptor potential. If this potential reduction becomes large enough, the neighboring axon membrane becomes depolarized and a series of spike potentials is propagated along the nerve. The different characteristics of the receptor and action potentials suggest that there may be a difference in the properties of the cell and axon membranes. The properties of the two types of membrane are as follows:

Axon membrane in the receptor	Axon membrane outside the receptor
1. Electric response: hypopolarization	Electric response: depolarization
2. Localized process	Propagating process
3. Correlation between signal intensity and hypopolarization (analog process)	"All-or-nothing" response (digital process)
4. No refractory state	Refractory state during the passing of the spike potential

The question arises how the external stimulus is converted into periodic impulses by the receptor, or, in cybernetic terms, how the *analog-to-digital conversion* comes about in the receptor. As has been seen, the receptor potential reflects

24

the intensity and duration of the stimulus: hypopolarization is proportional to the strength of the incoming signal and lasts as long as there is stimulation. That is why we might call the electrical response of the receptor an analog process which conforms to the parameters of the stimulus.

The "all-or-nothing" nature of nerve signals is found if the electrical changes are studied at any part of the peripheral afferent nervous pathway. It might be concluded therefore that the analog-to-digital conversion, i.e., transcription of the received information (encoding), is accomplished in the receptor. The nervous impulse is then transmitted to the central neurons in this transcribed form, which makes transmission and probably also storing easier (see p. 212). **Site of transcription**

Information is generally understood to mean items of knowledge or news about some event or change. In this sense nervous impulses conducted from the peripheral receptors to the brain transmit information in the same way as pulses traveling along telephone cables or radio waves. The greater the probability of an event, the more valuable is the information relating to it. By the use of probability theory, information can be measured and expressed numerically. The *bit* is the unit of the information content of a message. This amount of information is obtained from a single yes-or-no decision, i.e., if the probability of an event is 0.5. Information theory is interested only in the quantitative aspects of information, leaving aside its meaning and importance. Neurophysiology, on the contrary, also deals with the quality of information, i.e., with the benefit the organism may derive from the message for its well-being and adaptation. **Information**

Messages are transmitted in the nervous system, as in communication systems in general, in the form of signals (codes). Transcription into a system of signals (encoding) facilitates the transmission and storing of information. It is a fundamental requirement of such systems that the **Encoding**

25

message be *decodeable* at the receiving end. Speaking about the nervous system one might say that encoding is performed in the receptors and decoding in the brain.

Binary code Encoding systems in which only two kinds of signals (0 and 1) are used are called binary systems. Information in the nervous system is probably transmitted by help of such a *binary code*. At least this is suggested by the "all-or-nothing" nature of nerve signals consisting of series of pulses the passage of which is followed by refractory periods.

Binary digits are also employed in computers for transmitting and storing information. The use of the binary number system which has been suggested by J. Neumann and others is practical because it makes it possible to employ simple and reliable electronic equipment.

Information channel A suitable medium is needed for the transmission of information. This is what we call *channels* (Fig. 3). Telephone cables and nerve axons might both be regarded as information channels. The *capacity* of such channels is defined as the maximum amount of information that can be transferred per unit of time. It is expressed in terms of bits per second. Signals entering the transmitting end of the system are called *input* signals, while those obtained at the receiving end are called *output* signals. In practice some of the information is lost during transmission because the input signals are distorted by various factors (called noise) interfering with the transfer of messages in the nervous system. This and the distortion of information at the nodes of Ranvier along the myelinated nerve fiber and elsewhere are problems of neurophysiology awaiting solution. It is probable that the distortions of the train of pulses transmitted as binary signals along nerve fiber are corrected by signals of other parallel-running fibers transmitting the same information. It has been pointed out by Neumann that the interference of parallel noisy channels yields favorable results statistically. The relatively poor insulation of the

26

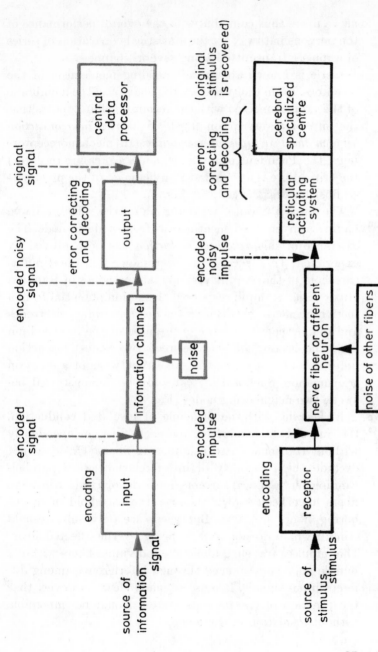

Fig. 3. Scheme of information transmission in communication systems (red) and in the nervous system (black).

nerve fibers thus contributes to the overall performance of the nervous pathway by the statistical correlation of series of impulses transmitted along several channels.

Little is known about the encoding mechanism of the receptors. From the two kinds of behavior of the membrane of the axon connected with the receptor cell it appears that the site of transcription must be at the *interconnection between the two types of membrane.* In mechanoreceptors (e.g., the Pacinian corpuscle, which is a pressure receptor) the critical site is at the first Ranvier node of the myelinated fiber leaving the cell (see Fig. 1).

Saltatory conduction
The binary impulse traveling along the afferent nerve having a myelinated sheath leaps from node to node. The existence of this *saltatory conduction* has been proved by experimental evidence. It has been shown that the stimulus threshold of the axon is very low at the nodes of Ranvier. Huxley and Stämpfli registered the action potential from a section of nerve between two nodes using microelectrodes and found that within the entire area of the internodium (i.e., the section of fiber between two nodes) the action potentials all appear at the same time without a delay in transmission. Such a delay can only be demonstrated between two neighboring nodes (Fig. 4).

Insulation of nerve fibers
In keeping with the principle of insulated conduction, the impulse is conducted by each fiber independently without transmission to neighboring fibers. This does not exclude the possibility of interference between parallel-running nerves. Local currents due to depolarization in nerve fibers have been shown to lower the threshold of neighboring fibers by 20%. But these are only subthreshold stimuli which do not lead to firing by the affected fiber. The impulses traveling along the individual fibers within a bundle may be weakened through interference among different input signals. It must be made clear, however, that the function of the nervous system would be impossible without insulation of the fibers.

28

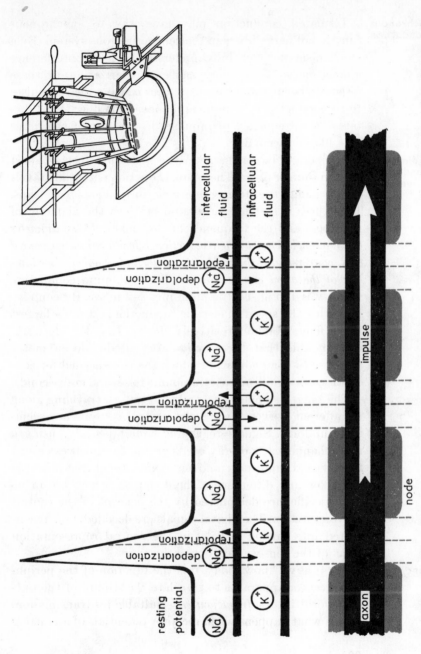

Fig. 4. Technique of registering the action potential (right upper corner) and saltatory transmission of impulses. Action potential can only be registered from the nodes of Ranvier, which are not covered with myelin sheath.

Synchronous conduction   Insulated conduction may give way to synchronous function of nerve fibers in the central nervous system. By a mechanism not yet fully understood, strong interference among nerve fibers may cause depolarization in these nerves to occur simultaneously, thus causing their impulses to be conducted in a uniform manner. The fiber that "dictates" the frequency of impulses in the rest of the fibres acts like a pacemaker.

Axon diameter and conduction velocity   In fibers of larger diameter the nodes are further apart than in thinner fibers. Therefore, the action potential travels faster along the former, having to make bigger leaps. Thus there is a strict correlation between the diameter of the fibers and the frequency of the spikes. *If the diameter of an axon is known, the conduction velocity can be computed and, conversely, if the conduction velocity is known, the diameter of the axon can be inferred.* The maximum conduction velocity is 120 m/sec, the minimum 1–2 m/sec. By comparison with the speed of electric conduction, even the largest nerve fibers conduct relatively slowly. It is therefore understandable that the *reaction time* needed for a motor response to come about, of which the time needed for conduction is a significant part, amounts to several milliseconds.

The binary signals, i.e., trains of pulses, traveling along the afferent nerves toward the central neurons are seemingly uniform. Signals registered simultaneously, using a multichannel cathode-ray oscillograph, from nerves arising from visual, auditory, and cutaneous touch receptors do not show any differences. These signals, which are in no way specific, are deciphered by the neurons of the central nervous system. The digital signals are decoded, i.e., reconverted into analog signals, in the central representation areas of the sensory nervous pathways.

Frequency code   As far as we know today, it is the function of the peripheral receptor apparatus to translate the stimuli of the outside world into a *frequency code* suitable for transmission. This is what happens when receptor potentials of an analog character, i.e., quantitatively related to the strength of the stimulus, are converted into action potentials of uniform amplitude and differing only in frequency (all-or-nothing). The frequency of the spikes thus stands in correlation with the intensity of the stimulus. This mechanism of receptor encoding, first suggested by Adrian, is still regarded as the basis of nervous conduction. It is, however, believed to be only one element of an *unknown system of codes*. The spatial integration of impulses traveling in separate fibers (which may have a stimulatory or inhibitory effect on one another) and the interference among the fibers may all be part of this system. Clarification of the function of the central decoding apparatus is one of the most intriguing problems of psychophysiology.

Functional unity of analyzers

It would be very difficult to draw an anatomical border between the peripheral (receiving) and central (data-processing) parts of analyzers. A solution of this problem can be expected only from phylogenetic research. All specialized sensory pathways consist of three to five neurons. Whereas the first two neurons of the optic pathway are still in the retina, i.e., on the periphery, the second neurons of pathways conveying sensory information from the skin or muscles are topographically already part of the central nervous system. In the following all processes of perception which take place in the central nervous system will be regarded as central, irrespective of the actual site of the process, which may be in the spinal cord, in the brain stem, or in the sophisticated cerebral neurons.

Center and periphery

Once more about the problem of methods

The dilemma of methods   We have already referred to the intricate problems of methodology when dealing with the function of the receptors. It is a well-known dilemma for both biologists and psychologists. The root of the problem lies in the fact that the function of living organisms can be studied at several levels from macromolecular processes to the behavior of the entire healthy organism. When studying the molecular processes of brain cells, the psychological aspects of brain function are lost and, the other way around, if we only deal with the external signs of behavior in keeping with the "black box" theory, nothing will be known about the biophysical, biochemical, and physiological background of these phenomena. The solution of the dilemma lies in the application of *complex* methods. This approach has been adopted by modern psychophysiological research. In the following, a short description of the most important physiological methods will be given since the different biophysical and biochemical techniques as well as the methods of classical psychology are not pertinent here.

Subjective report   The classical methods of the research of sense organ function are the psychophysical ones, which were already applied by the first investigators of this field (Johannes Müller, Weber, etc.). Analysis of the correlations between the physical characteristics of external stimuli and subjective sensation was, in those days, an important novel approach and is, with certain restrictions, still applicable today. It is a common characteristic of psychophysical methods that they rely on the subjective report of the test subject. These methods are, in fact, indispensable because they make use of verbal report, i.e., human introspection, representing a unique approach to certain aspects of psychological processes. Similar or identical subjective experience gained through introspection from a large group of test

32

subjects may, in fact, be regarded as objective data. The subjective report is, at the same time, a common drawback of psychophysical methods. The numerous sources of error involved in the use of introspection are well known. These are due to the lability of the information gained in this way as well as to the high number of different psychological and somatic factors influencing the overall result. The same picture or sound is perceived differently by the same person depending on whether he is tired or rested, in a happy mood or distressed. The result is again different if he is excited. In view of these shortcomings, it is easily understandable that time and again there have been tendencies both in psychology and neurophysiology to eliminate these methods. The sceptical attitudes of the American behaviorists as well as of certain representatives of the Pavlovian school are well known.

It must be clear from the foregoing that the psychophysical methods are a useful, sometimes indispensable, approach to be applied when studying the relations between stimuli and sensation (see later).

Nevertheless, the *objective methods* which belong to the realm of biology are given preference in the study of perception. Several such methods are known and are mostly used in conjunction with each other, one making up for the shortcomings of the next.

Extirpation of the brain is a method that had already been **Extirpation** known to Galen. Changes in sensory organ function are observed following the removal or destruction of some brain areas. From the results conclusions may be drawn about the involvement of the affected cerebral area in the regulation of sensory function. It was pointed out by Pavlov, however, that this method is inaccurate because the experimental lesion also affects neighboring structures and their function. Placement of lesions in the deeper layers of cerebral substance is facilitated by the use of the techniques of *stereotaxis*, first introduced by Horsley and Clarke **Stereotaxis**

(Fig. 5). By this method an exact map of any desired brain area can be made and the data obtained can be exactly specified with respect to well-definable points of the skull (e.g., the inferior edge of the orbit). A metal framework is clamped to the skull of the animal and an electrode mounted on this framework is inserted through a previously drilled hole in the skull. The electrode can be moved along the frame in all directions, and with the help of the map the electrode can be brought into position inside the head at any desired point that can be specified by three coordinates. The electrode thus placed can be used for either destruction or stimulation of the given area. Stereotactic maps have been made of the brains of almost all animal species used for neurophysiological research, indicating that the dimensions of the skull and brain of adult rats, guinea pigs, monkeys, etc. are exactly the same. The stereotactic technique is also applied in brain surgery for therapeutic purposes. In these cases, the fixed points facilitating orientation are selected brain structures.

Stimulation   The method of stimulation was first applied by Fritsch and Hitzig in the nineteenth century. They applied chemical or electric stimuli to some part of the perceptive apparatus and observed the objective and subjective changes ensuing in response to stimulation. Electric current is especially suitable for stimulation. Not only can its intensity and duration be exactly controlled, but the "shape" of the pulses, i.e., the speed of the voltage change can also be regulated. Rectangular pulses, which have a steep upstroke and allow the sudden termination of stimulation, are the most advantageous type of electric stimuli.

Conditioned reflex   Observation and recording of the behavior of experimental animals became a standard objective method of the study of sense organ function as early as the beginning of the twentieth century. Pavlov described the method of conditioned reflexes, providing a useful tool for—among others—the study of sense organs. The limits of the perceptive and

34

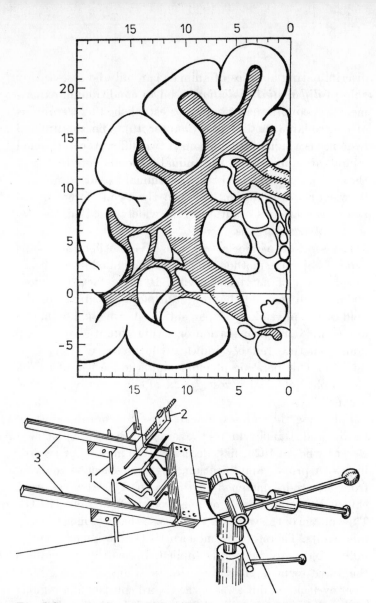

Fig. 5. Stereotactic map with millimeter scale (top); and schematic drawing of a stereotaxis apparatus (bottom). The head of the anaesthetized animal is clamped within the metal frame having two parallel bars (3). The frame is fixed to the ears by metal spikes (1). The electrode holder (2) is placed on the bars. It has a millimeter scale and can be moved in all directions. By its help the electrode can be inserted and brought into position inside the skull.

discriminating abilities of animals can only be assessed by help of *differential inhibition*, used in conditioning experiments. A conditioned response is established to a stimulus of controllable quality (see Chapter 10). The conditioned response is a sign of perception. If two different conditioned stimuli are applied and the animal responds only to one of these, it may be inferred that the animal has discriminated between the stimuli, i.e., between the two different qualities of sensation. Conditioning is widely used in the research of sense organs.

Bioelectric activity   Registration of bioelectric signals is another important type of objective method which can be applied in the study of all levels of nervous activity. It is, in fact, the most widely used method, having multiple applications in the field of the physiology of perception. As we have seen, the appearance and propagation of action potentials in a nervous structure reliably indicate the presence of nervous impulse. This periodic phenomenon is made use of in the electrophysiological investigation of the function of sense organs.

Electroencephalography   Following the independent discovery of brain waves by Caton and Danilevski in the nineteenth century, it was Berger who, in 1929, first described the method of recording, with proper amplification, rhythmic electric activity from electrodes fastened to the scalp. These waves were called Berger's waves or electroencephalogram (EEG). The voltage of the waves is very low so that it is measured in microvolts. Therefore, in modern EEG equipment several-millionfold amplification is applied. In healthy individuals the wave form is characteristic. In subjects resting with their eyes closed but awake, the record consists of a regular series of sinusoidal waves, called the *alpha rhythm*. It has a frequency of 8 to 10 per second and a voltage of 50 μV. The alpha rhythm is strongest if picked up from the back of the head. If the subject is told to open his eyes or is made alert in some other way, the record will diminish in ampli-

36

tude but increase in frequency (13 to 30 per second). This pattern, characteristic of the alert state, is called *beta activity*. From the point of view of sense organ function, it is the alpha and beta rhythms which are of interest, more precisely, the transition from resting alpha rhythm to beta activity. The third wave type, called *delta rhythm*, is registered if the subject is asleep. Its long slow waves have an amplitude generally over 50 μV and a frequency lower than 4 per second.

If a subject resting with eyes closed is exposed to an unexpected stimulus, the alpha rhythm will give way to another pattern, i.e., alpha blockade (depression of the alpha rhythm) will occur. The transition to beta activity, i.e., to higher frequency, indicates that the sensory impulse evoked by the exogenous stimulus has reached an important area of the central nervous system. A more detailed description of this phenomenon will be given in Chapter 7. Here it should only be noted that alpha blockade (or desynchronization) can be used as an objective test of perception.

Alpha blockade

A more important electrophysiological method for the study of sensory function is that of *evoked potentials* (Fig. 6), which has increasingly been used over the past decades. It has long been known that if a receptor apparatus or sensory nerve is stimulated, a well-recognizable response can be recorded from certain groups of neurons of the corresponding central area. This response may be seen in the EEG record as a biphasic curve consisting of a very large (up to 500 μV) positive wave and a subsequent negative wave. It can be sharply delimited from the pattern of "spontaneous" firing of the normal EEG. This specific response to a stimulus, caused by the specific impulse traveling along the specialized sensory pathway, is called the evoked potential. Unlike the normal EEG waves, this "high-voltage" potential can only be recorded from circumscribed areas of cerebral representation and only in

Evoked potentials

37

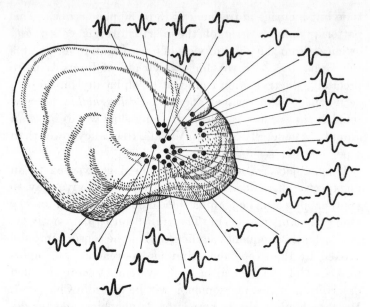

Fig. 6. Map made by the evoked potential method from the sensory areas of the cat brain. The cortical topography of interoceptive sensory impulses originating from internal organs is shown.

response to appropriate sensory impulses. It is important to note that evoked potentials are secured only from cells along the sensory pathway, i.e., from the cortical and subcortical sensory areas.

Brain maps Owing to these properties, the evoked potentials may be used for mapping the sensory centers of the brain. For example, evoked potentials may be recorded from the exposed brain of experimental animals in the following way. An auditory stimulus is applied and the exploring electrode is moved millimeter by millimeter along the auditory cortex. In this manner the points showing the largest voltage and the shortest latency can be found. These points can be regarded as the central representations of the stimulated auditory organ.

38

Evoked potentials from both the cortex and deeper structures (diencephalon, mesencephalon) may be attributed to the summation of the local hypopolarization waves of neurons.

Registration of certain physiological changes should also be mentioned among the objective methods of studying sensory function. It is well known to physiologists that perception is accompanied by a number of changes involving the body as a whole. Unexpected environmental stimuli may cause changes in blood pressure (elevation or depression), respiration (increased or decreased respiratory rate), fine alterations in gastrointestinal function, etc. Naturally, these changes are not so strong as to cause considerable disturbances in the function of the body, but when followed with the help of sensitive instruments they may be objective indicators of perception. Among the major physiological changes and indices which are most frequently studied we may mention blood pressure, respiratory rate and depth, heart rate, and the electrical resistance of the skin, which is measured using a special apparatus. The changes in skin resistance thus recorded are most probably due to alterations in the function of sweat glands in the skin.

We thought it appropriate to deal with the objective biological methods of examining central nervous mechanisms before we embark upon the discussion of sensory functions because the reader should be made aware of the possibilities and limitations in this field. So far no uniform scheme of examination methods has been evolved which would make possible a complex and reliable survey of parallel peripheral and central events.

Connection between stimulus and perception

The problem of decoding It is a well-known problem of natural sciences that while we have a relatively good knowledge of the *individual mechanisms* within a system, the *general principles* of the function of the system as a whole are not known. This is also true of psychology, as will be seen repeatedly in subsequent chapters. The greatest problem in the field of sensory function is decoding. It has been shown that in the receptor cell an analog signal (electric potential) is generated by external stimuli. This analog message is encoded in the nerve fiber, i. e., it is translated into a digital frequency code, which is then transmitted toward the central neurons. The message is undoubtedly decoded by the appropriate central structures. Unfortunately, however, the rules of this decoding process are not known. All we suspect is that—to adopt the jargon of communication engineering once more—a *digital-to-analog conversion* must occur in the central structures. Thus, a "sandwich-like" process occurs in the course of which the original message is twice converted. That the end result is an analog response is substantiated not only by common experience but also by scientific argument as will be shown later on.

A growing body of data is becoming available on certain mechanisms within the central decoding system. Several cortical and subcortical groups of neurons are known which are specialized for the perception of color or form in the process of vision, for that of pitch and timbre in audition, or for sensing changes in speed and direction of movements. There are separate cells in the control centers for the perception of individual colors and forms or for changes in the position of the extremities, etc.

Primary sensory systems When studying the relation between stimuli and perception, the problem of primary sensory qualities should be mentioned. Undoubtedly, there exist specific sensory

40

pathways and separate senses like vision, audition, taste, and smell, but the number of primary sensory systems cannot be exactly defined as yet. In constrast to the traditional "five senses," scientific research has revealed the existence of a much higher number of sensory systems. These were described with the help of the already mentioned subjective and objective methods as early as the end of the nineteenth century. Nevertheless, a number of unanswered problems remained. For instance, a number of cold, warm, touch, pressure, and pain receptors are known in the skin which, according to the notions of classical physiology, perceive their specific stimuli separately. The specific sensitivity of individual receptors described by anatomists and pathologists long ago has, however, recently been challenged. It has been found that certain touch and pressure receptors in the skin are also sensitive to chemical and, occasionally, to heat stimuli. Similarly, there is evidence available refuting the specificity of interoceptors, receptors situated in internal organs.

Classification of the sense organs also reflects these uncertainties. According to the classical theory of Sherrington, a distinction can be made between exteroceptors responding to stimuli of the environment and interoceptors transmitting information relating to the state of the inner organs. However, it is difficult to draw a line between the two classes of receptors, and the problems become even more numerous when it comes to classification within these categories. For instance, what is the place of the taste receptors of the mouth within this system? Are the chemoreceptors of the taste buds to be regarded as extero- or interoceptors? In such cases only arbitrary distinctions can be made, which are mostly formal, relating to the terminology only. It is much more important to decide whether these receptors are able to respond exclusively to chemical stimuli, or whether they are also sensitive to mechanical impacts. This question has not yet been unequivocally answered by neurophysiological

41

research. The classification most frequently applied is submitted in the table below, but the above-mentioned shortcomings of this system must be stressed.

Classification of receptors according to the kind of stimulus
(after Sherrington)

According to the position of the source of stimulus in relation to the organism	According to the type of physical energy

Exteroceptors:
  telereceptors
  contact receptors
	Photoreceptors
	Mechanoreceptors
	  (auditory, vestibular,
	    and cutaneous receptors)
	Thermoreceptors
	Chemoreceptors

Interoceptors:
  proprioceptors
  visceroceptors
	Mechanoreceptors
	Chemoreceptors
	Thermoreceptors
	Osmoreceptors

Psychophysical principles   The advantages and shortcomings of psychophysical methods have already been referred to. A long line of important conclusions have been drawn from them, such as, e. g., *Weber's law*. This law, written as $\Delta I/I = K$, states that the fraction of two stimuli producing a noticeable difference in perception is constant. It applies equally to cutaneous sensation, vision, audition, and other senses.

Fechner based his speculations on Weber's law. He assumed a logarithmic relation between stimulus and sensation, i.e.,

$$\psi = k \cdot \log \varphi$$

where φ is the intensity of the stimulus and ψ the strength of the sensation. In other words, this means that the sensation varies directly with the *logarithm* of the stimulus. The insufficiency of *Fechner's law* has recently been proved by up-to-date research applying psychophysical and electrophysiological methods. Stevens, among others, has suggested the following formula:

$$\psi = k \cdot \varphi^n$$

expressing the relation between stimulus and sensation in terms of an exponential equation. The value of n varies with the kind of stimulus, e. g., it is 0.3 for auditory stimuli, 3.5 for electric cutaneous stimuli, etc. It might justifiably be asked how we can accept a numerically expressed correlation between two variables of which one, the stimulus, is readily measurable while the registration of the other, sensation, depends on subjective factors, and this in the face of our criticism of the precision of the introspective method. The answer lies in the great number of experimental subjects used in these series and the statistical methods used for the evaluation of the results. If the subjective reports of a large number of subjects all suggest the same conclusion, the method can be regarded as objective. The usefulness of the laws of Fechner and Stevens has recently been substantiated by electrophysiological investigations. For example, Mountcastle and co-workers have found a similar exponential relation between the frequency of impulses transmitted by the receptors of the skin and muscles and the intensity of the external stimulus (e.g., degree of skin deformation). A direct relation between impulse frequency—a digital signal—and some power of stimulus intensity has been confirmed by various research workers using light and sound stimuli.

Physiological characteristics of perception

Gestalt and behaviorist theories

Our present views on the process of perception have evolved from two opposing theories. One of these is known as the *Gestalt theory*. Adherents of this school of thought maintained that complexes of external stimuli rather than individual stimuli are perceived by the animal and human nervous system, e.g., the shape, color, and movement of an object are perceived as a single sensation and not separately by separate senses. In sharp distinction to this theory, the *behaviorists* proclaimed the existence of elementary sensory function only, attributing the synthesizing ability to the brain alone. Modern physiology has attempted to reconcile these two extreme theories by supposing that perception is, in fact, more complicated than a series of elementary discriminations, but less complex than the "all at once" sensation postulated by the Gestalt theory. The final solution most probably will be a gradual synthesis at several levels between these two hypotheses.

Multidimensional character

Undoubtedly, the function of perception is not just the arrival of trains of impulses at central neurons. There must be a complex process of analysis and synthesis in the central structures, giving perception a multidimensional character. Perception must be more complex than the eliciting stimulus. This, naturally, does not contradict the philosophical notion of reflection, but rather stresses the role of subjective factors in the nervous reactions to objective external stimuli. Several examples could be listed here such as the phenomenon known as the Bezold-Brücke's illusion, namely, that different hues are perceived for the same object under changing illumination, or the observation that low-frequency tones are perceived as having a lower pitch at high stimulus intensities than they are thought to have at low stimulus intensities. While physiologists at the beginning of our century attempted to eliminate such "illusions",

44

they are a problem of distinct interest to researchers today.

Organization is another important characteristic of sensory function. The brain is able to discriminate environmental stimulus complexes which seem to belong together, i.e., show some degree of organization, and to select them from among a mass of redundant information. Using the terminology of communication systems, the signal-from-noise selection of the sensory apparatus is very effective. The mechanism of this *selectivity* is still unknown. **Organization**

Selectivity

The ability to perform *transpositions* is an important property of the sensory apparatus. Perception is always relative — no absolute discrimination between stimuli is possible. Nevertheless, discrimination of what is called psychological dimensions can be transferred to a series of stimuli of different intensity. Transposition makes it possible for stimulus complexes of similar organization but different composition to be recognized as similar. For instance, the ability to transpose is used when the same letter is recognized in different handwritings or the same tune is identified when played by different instruments. **Transposition**

The importance of previous experience in perception must be given due consideration. Innate reactions and learned abilities are equally important constituents of perceptual activity. It will be seen, for instance, that visual depth perception is a learned ability absent in the brain of newborn babies. Now we have learned about the complexity of the process of perception from the analog-to-digital conversion in the receptor apparatus to the central decoding of the rhythmic train of impulses. **Experience**

The transmission of information to central structures, i.e., afferentation, is not the only task of the sensory apparatus. Through what we call *central control* the receptors are instructed by the central nervous system. These instructions controlling the sensitivity of the receptors reach the receptor cells by efferent pathways. The function of efferent **Central control** fibers running to the retina of the eye were described by Granit, while those connecting the brain with the receptor structures of the inner ear were described by Galambos, among others.

The recognition of the central control of sense organs also has philosophical implications. Contrary to earlier views regarding mental functions as being rigidly determined by stimuli of the external environment, the existence of a more complex—we might say, more dialectical—relation between the brain and the environment has been recognized. In light of these modern views on mental activity, sensation is seen as an *active* process in which both afferent and efferent elements are involved.

Chapter 2

Perception of electromagnetic waves: vision

The adequate stimulus of the retina of the eyes is the visible spectrum of electromagnetic waves ranging in wavelength from 400 to 800 nm. Within this range the individual wavelengths are perceived as different colors (Fig. 7).

In response to light stimuli, the receptor cells of the retina send trains of periodic impulses to the central nervous system. Let us follow this process from the retina to the visual cortex.

The receiving end: the retina

The retina has a highly complicated structure. It consists of ten layers and might be regarded as an outpost nervous center because the greatest part of its tissue is made up of nerve cells. It differs from all other sense organs in this respect. From the point of view of perception three types of retinal cells are of importance.

Structure of the retina

The first are the *receptor cells*, the rods and cones. There are no rods in the fovea centralis, which is in the center of

47

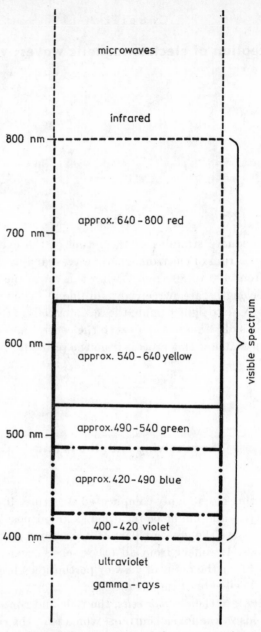

Fig. 7. The visible spectrum of electromagnetic waves.

48

the macula lutea opposite the pupil, but toward the periphery the rods become more numerous, in proportion to the cones (Fig. 8). The retina of the human eye contains about 120 million rods and 6 million cones. It is remarkable that in addition to passing through the optic system of the eye (cornea, anterior chamber, pupil, lens, vitreous humor), light also has to traverse the layers of the retina before reaching the light-sensitive apparatus. The rods and cones are not directly connected with the optic nerve running to the brain. They form synaptic junctions with the *bipolar cells* making up the layer of neurons. A single receptor cell may be connected with several bipolar cells and, conversely, several receptor cells may enter into synaptic connection with a single bipolar cell. This allows a wide range of variations to occur. The bipolar cells, in their turn, feed into *ganglion cells*, the fibers of which join to form the optic nerve. The connections between bipolar and ganglion cells are likewise manifold. The totality of rods and/or cones connected with the optic nerve through a single ganglion cell (through the mediation of bipolar cells) is called a *receptor field*. The impulses are carried to the brain by the fibers of about 1 million ganglion cells from approximately 130 million receptor cells. The proportion being about 130 : 1, there is need for strong convergence.

Differentiation of light stimuli, i.e., the elementary processes of form and color perception, starts at this end of the visual pathway.

It has long been known that, if the optical system of the eye is normal, the *visual acuity* of the human retina is about 1 minute, which means that the eye sees two points as separate if they subtend an angle of at least 1 minute at the fovea, the point of sharpest vision. It has been shown that there must be a "silent" cone between two stimulated cones in this case. This corresponds to a retinal distance of 4 μm (the average diameter of the cones is 3 μm).

It has been shown by recent studies that the behavior of

Visual acuity

ON and OFF cells

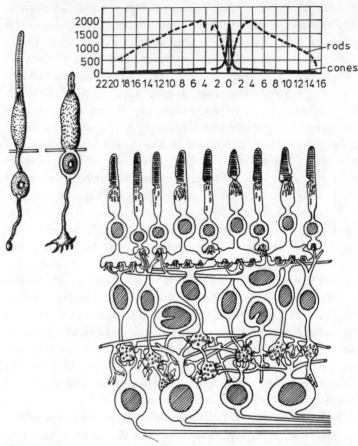

Fig. 8. Structure of the retina with rods and cones. The scheme, drawn after electron micrographs, shows the thicker cones and thinner rods in the upper layer. The rods and cones are connected with the bipolar cells of the middle layer, which, in turn, are connected with the ganglion cells of the bottom layer. The axons of the ganglion cells form the visual pathway. The morphology of a rod and a cone is shown diagrammatically on the left, while the curves above show the distribution of the rods and cones over the retina. Ordinate, number of receptor elements; abscissa, distance from the fovea (marked as 0) in millimeters.

50

the individual receptor cells stimulated by a beam of light is not uniform. Kuffler measured the action potential of ganglion cells by inserting microelectrodes into the eyes of various mammals. He found that the light stimulus increased the resting activity of some of the cells, while it decreased that of other cells (rhythmic spontaneous firing of

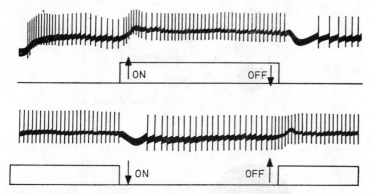

Fig. 9. Diagram of action potential changes of an ON cell (top), and OFF cell (bottom), in response to turning the light source on and off.

unstimulated receptor cells has been observed). This means that some cells are turned on by the light stimulus, while others are turned off (Fig. 9). Accordingly, the two types of cells are called ON and OFF elements, respectively. It is remarkable that the ON elements are always surrounded by circles of OFF elements, and the other way around (Fig. 10). This mosaic arrangement of stimulating and inhibiting elements in the retina ensures the primary processing of visual information in the eye. If two ON elements are illuminated, the impulses are summed before being transmitted over the visual pathway. However, if one bright spot illuminates an ON cell and the other an OFF element, the two opposite impulses neutralize each other and it may happen that no information is transmitted to the brain.

Diffuse illumination of the *entire* retina gives rise to much
less intensive impulses than stimulation with light beams
illuminating circumscribed areas of the retina. This presumably is the result of the sharply delineated mosaic
arrangement of ON and OFF cells in the retina and indicates that the visual receptors are most sensitive to *contrast*.

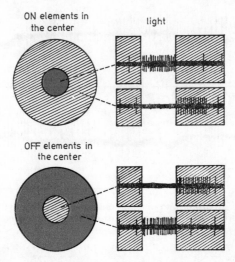

Fig. 10. Concentric arrangement of ON (red) and OFF (striated)
elements in the retina and the corresponding action potentials
(after Hubel).

The resolving power of the retina is highest in the fovea
because here the closely packed cones may each constitute
a receptor field (i. e., be connected to a single ganglion
cell). Thus foveal visual acuity is 1 minute (4 μm), in contrast to the periphery, where the diameter of a single receptor field may be several millimeters, corresponding to a
visual acuity of 3 degrees.

In some mammals (e. g., in the rabbit) the frequency of
the transmitted impulses varies with the *direction* of moving
light. The same has not been proved for either man or high-

er mammals like the cat or monkey. These detectors sensitive to movement have only been demonstrated in the brain.

The phenomenon of *critical fusion frequency* is connected C. f. f. effect with an important property of the retina. Intermittent light is seen as steady, i. e., flickers are fused, above certain frequencies. Early investigations of c. f. f., the frequency at which flickering disappears, used a rotating wheel composed of transparent and opaque sections and a light source placed behind it. Now an electronically controlled stroboscope producing flickers at the required frequency is used for this purpose. Although c. f. f. is a cortical function, the retina undoubtedly plays a role in bringing about fusion. It has been found that the frequency of electrical responses measured in the ganglion cells of the eye of experimental animals follows the frequency of the flickers of the light source. Above a critical frequency the response ceases to be analog and only a single ganglion potential is produced. This means that the single receptor cells have their own c. f. f. It has been supposed that fusion in the brain is based on the elementary c. f. f. of the retinal receptor cells.

The phenomena described so far had nothing to do with the wavelength of light, i.e., with color. The sensitivity of the different retinal receptors to different wavelengths varies, and therefore retinal processes are important from the point of view of *color vision*.

It has long been recognized by physiologists studying Duplicity theory sense organs as well as by ophthalmologists that the two types of receptor cells of the retina, i. e., the rods and the cones, differ in their functional characteristics. The cones serve sharp vision in daylight and respond to differences in wavelength. On the other hand, the rods have the function of light-dark discrimination, thus serving for night vision and reception of dim light. The stimulus threshold of rods is lower, and with the help of a special photochemical process (see below), the light sensitivity of the retina increases in darkness. This function is called *dark adaptation*. In the dark-adapted eye the sensitivity of the retina approximates the highest possible value: the lowest threshold of the rods is a single quantum of radiant energy (light). Having this fantastic light sensitivity, the rods do not respond to wavelength differences; color detection is the function of the cones, which in turn have a much lower light sensitivity (minimum threshold, 5–7 quanta). There are only cones in the fovea, where a single cone may constitute a receptor field, as has been noted above. Toward the periphery the number of rods increases. Thus vision is based on the joint function of two receptor types at the receiving end, as indicated by the duplicity theory.

Photochemical processes   In both the rods and the cones the generation of a receptor potential leading to impulse formation is preceded by specific photochemical events. There is a substance, *rhodopsin*, called visual purple, in the rods, which is broken down by light (one quantum is needed for the breakdown of one molecule). The breakdown products play a role in the generation of the receptor potential. The process is reversible and the breakdown products, retin and opsin, are reconstituted into visual purple in response to darkness. Similar substances may also be found in the cones, but their breakdown mechanism is not well understood. According to Wald, three kinds of light-sensitive dyes are found in three different groups of cones. Some cones contain pigment which is sensitive to green light, while others show sensitivity to red and blue light, respectively. This finding supports the *three-color (trichomatic) theory* of Young proposed as early as 1801. According to this, the perception of the approximately 160 hues which human vision is able to differentiate is

Dominators and modulators   the result of single or summed impulses of three kinds of receptors, each sensitive to a well-defined wavelength, i.e., color. The three-color theory was substantiated by the experiments of Granit, who, using the microelectrode technique,

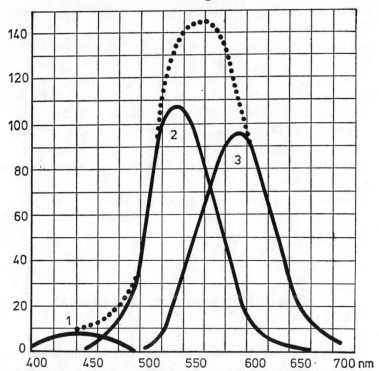

Fig. 11. Sensitivity curves of dominators (D) and modulators (1, 2, 3), the latter showing sensitivity to different wavelengths.

was able to pick up action potentials from the retinal ganglion cells of the cat. He found that in both the dark-adapted and light-adapted retina, the majority of cells (mainly the rods) are sensitive to a wide spectrum of wavelengths and respond with firing to such stimuli. The sensitivity curve of the retina is dominated by this single response to all colors, called *dominator* response by Granit. There is, however, a smaller group of retinal ganglion cells firing only in response to one of the three basic colors. These ganglion cells connected with the receptor fields of cones are

55

called *modulators*. They modify the impulses fired by the dominators according to the wavelength of the light perceived (Fig. 11).

As we have seen, the retina is an important member of the light-perceptive apparatus. The impulses arising in response to light stimuli of the visible spectrum are selected and grouped here, the contours are topographically arranged, and the color sensations modulated before being transmitted to the brain. The 130 million receptor elements are connected with 1 million ganglion cells and the corresponding axons. These are the elements of a complex encoding system supplying information to the even more complex transmitting and decoding system.

The thalamus—a central relay station

After leaving the retina the fibers of the ganglion cells join to form the optic nerve or optic pathway running to the thalamus. Half of the fibers of the visual pathway cross over on the brainstem. Thus both cerebral hemispheres receive fibers from both retinas (Figs 12 and 13). The thalamus, which is a large mass of neurons, is a relay station for *all* sensory pathways except for the olfactory nerve. The fibers of the visual pathway synapse with the cells of the lateral geniculate body (LGB) found at the posterior part of the thalamus. The evoked potential method (see above) has been applied for mapping the retinal projection areas of the LGB, and it has been found that each retinal area is represented by a corresponding point in the thalamus.

The role of the thalamic neurons in light perception is not known. Animals deprived of their cerebral cortex, i.e., possessing only the thalamus, retain an elementary capacity of light perception, but are incapable of recognition and differentiation of stimuli (objects, food).

Microelectrode studies of the thalamic cells have revealed **ON and OFF** ON and OFF cells arranged similarly to those found in the **fields**

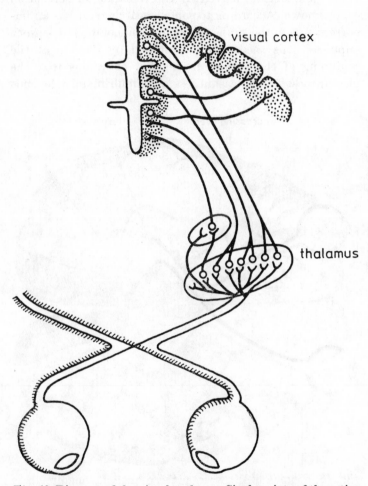

visual cortex

thalamus

Fig. 12. Diagram of the visual pathway. Single points of the retina are represented by corresponding sites in the thalamus and visual cortex.

retina, with the difference that the ON elements are even more sharply delimited from the surrounding OFF cells. Thus the possibilities of differentiation between diffuse illumination and sharp contours are even more evident at this level of the visual system.

The general part played by the thalamus in perception is not known. According to some researchers, it has an important role in the subjective emotional coloring of sensory impulses. This theory, first proposed by Cannon at the beginning of the twentieth century, maintains that the pleasantness or unpleasantness of stimuli mainly depends

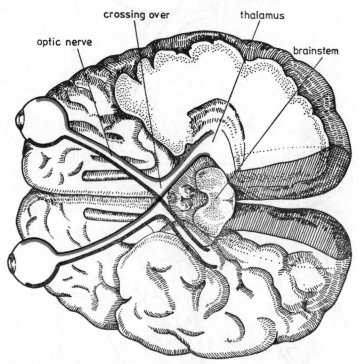

Fig. 13. Diagram of the visual pathway projected onto the base of the brain. Some of the fibers arising from the retina run to the thalamus without crossing, while others cross over. The striated area represents the visual cortex.

on the function of the thalamus. The close connection of the thalamus with the sensory cortex (see below) suggests the unity of the thalamic-cortical sensory function.

The cortical decoding center

The visual areas were among the first parts of the cerebral cortex to become known to physiologists. Gennari described the existence of the visual cortex in 1776. Its structure, extension, and microscopic and gross appearance are now accurately known. Some of the physiological functional properties of the visual cortex have also been clarified, but the decoding process as a whole, i.e., the complex function of visual perception, is still not completely understood. The few details of this complex mechanism that have become known in recent years, mainly due to extensive microphysiological research, are at the same time encouraging and challenging.

Almost all examination methods mentioned in Chapter 1 have been applied in the study of the cortical projection zone of the retina. In monkeys it has been found in the posterior part of the occipital lobe, and anatomical, neurosurgical, as well as neurological observations suggest that it occupies the same position in the human brain (Fig. 14). The fovea is represented by an area of a few square millimeters on the outer, convex surface of the lobe. Stimulation of a single retinal point by light or electric pulses results in evoked potentials at *several*, but at least *two*, cortical points.

In distinction to the relatively uniform organization of the LGB, the visual cortex is made up of several layers.

Visual cortex

59

The fibers of the LGB terminate in the fourth of the six layers distinguishable under the microscope, counting inward from the cortical surface. There is a rich network of fibers carrying information from this layer to adjacent ones. The third and fifth layers emit numerous fibers running to subcortical neurons and neighboring cortical areas.

It is a remarkable feature of this system that the number of vertical, columnar connections between the individual layers is much higher than the number of horizontal, lateral connections. It follows from this organization that individual retinal receptor fields have circumscribed vertical columns as projections in the cortex. This columnar organization has been confirmed by electrophysiological studies.

Columns of orientation Not long ago it was found by Hubel and Wiesel that all the neurons of these *cortical columns* are responsive to the same type of simple line stimuli, i.e., straight lines of illumination (slits or edges of contrast) with a specific orientation. For instance, if a cat is shown a vertical line in a white field, high-frequency action potentials can be recorded from

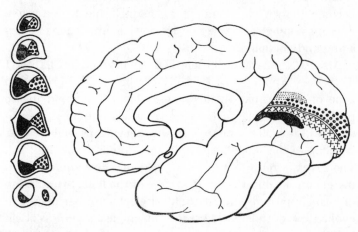

Fig. 14. Scheme of retinal projections on the medial portion of the visual cortex (right) and on sections of the lateral geniculate body of the thalamus (left). The areas marked with crosses and small dots on the cortex correspond to white areas in the LGB.

the appropriate cortical cells. Changing the orientation of the line, however, results in the disappearance of the cortical electrical response from these cells (Fig. 15). Cells of other columns respond to lines of other orientations. In this way a set of orientation columns containing all the specificities in a 180° arc (a "hypercolumn") has been postulated as a fundamental analytical unit. On the other hand, the complexity of responses has been found to vary with depth from the cortical surface, indicating the presence of several layers of simple and more complex cells. Cells responding to simple line stimuli (slits, edges or dark bars) have been called "simple" cells, while those responding to stimuli of composite configuration and to moving light have been called "complex" cells.

"Simple" and "complex" cells

ON and OFF cells may also be found in the visual cortex, but they are not concentrically arranged. The two kinds of cells are sharply delineated, and the direction of the dividing line depends on the orientation specificity of the neurons (Fig. 16). The function of orientation columns has been supposed to be mediated by lateral inhibition.

The distribution of the columnar functional units over the visual cortex is not uniform. "Simple" cells have been found to dominate in Brodmann's area 17 constituting the center of the visual cortex, whereas in areas 18 and 19 "complex" cells have been found to be more frequent. It has been suggested that the information analyzed and processed by simple cells is transmitted to complex cells for further analysis. It is thus probable that visual perception is the result of the cooperation of different cells.

Information encoded, analyzed, and processed in the retina and thalamus is decoded by the several million neurons of the cortex. The end result is thus an analog message, in accordance with the principle of environmental reflection. A third class of cells in the visual cortex has also been described, namely, the *"hypercomplex"* cells. These are true integrating units having a synthesizing function within the

"Hypercomplex" neurons

61

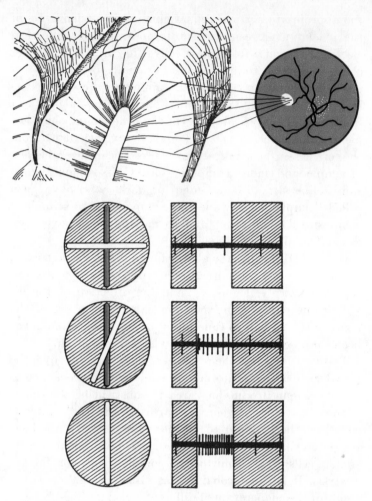

Fig. 15. Columnar organization of the cells of the cortical retinal projection (top) and scheme of the orientation-specific response of simple cortical cells (bottom). No action potential response is obtained by stimulation with a horizontal line from a cell responding specifically to vertical stimuli. The frequency of the response increases as the line is rotated and approaches the vertical position.

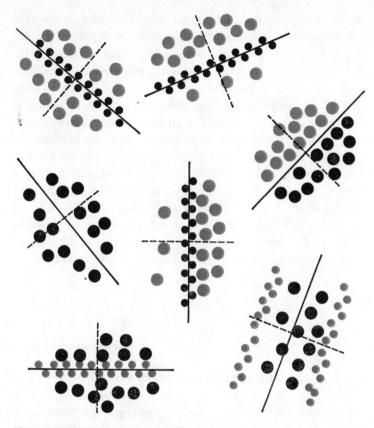

Fig. 16. Different orientation of the receptive fields of "simple" cortical cells. ON cells (red) are sharply delineated from OFF cells (black). The direction of the dividing line corresponds to the orientation to which the field shows sensitivity. The diameter of the receptive field is about 1 mm in the cat.

visual system. They are supplied with information by the lower neurons and ensure the uniformity of space and form perception.

These electrophysiological data, although providing a sound basis for further studies on the working of the brain, are insufficient for the interpretation of perception in the

63

terms of psychology. A large number of questions are still unanswered. To cite a relatively simple example, very little **Color perception** is known about the *color-perceiving function* of the brain. It seems certain that the message is encoded by the dominator-modulator system of the retina, but data are lacking as regards the processing and decoding activity in the LGB and cortex. Various types of neurons responding to different color stimuli have been investigated in the monkey thalamus, but the results are controversial. The reason for the scarcity of data is that the laboratory mammals (rodents, cats, monkeys) are poor color perceivers. The dog, for example, is unable to differentiate between colors. Most of the available information is based on experiments with frogs, and although these experiments were ingenious and very important, the results could not be transferred to man.

The central control of vision

The interaction of afferent and efferent mechanisms is more evident in the case of visual perception than in the case of any other sensory function. *Sensory* fibers running from the retina to the brain and *motor* fibers carrying impulses from the brain to the eye are *both* needed for the visual sensation to come about. There is no vision without central control, i.e., without the regulation by the brain of the movements of the peripheral sensory apparatus. Three kinds of efferent mechanisms are known.

Pupillary reflex The best known example of the cerebral regulatory function is the light reflex of the pupil. The sensory input is carried by the afferent limb of the reflex arc, the optic nerve, from the retina to the brain. Fibers of this type form separate bundles on the brainstem and run to a specific group of mesencephalic neurons (the Edinger–Westphal nucleus), where a connection is established with the efferent nerves regulating the constriction of the pupils in accordance with the intensity and distance of the light source. In this way the size of the pupil and the amount of light that may enter the eye in the following thousandth of a second are determined by the stimulus itself. The pupillary reflex is an important means of eliminating the "noise" from visual environmental information. If the reflex is blocked by atropine or some other drug having a paralyzing effect on the muscles constricting the pupils, there will be a decrease in visual acuity, and the perception of form and color will be impaired as well.

The function of the muscles ensuring the movement of the eyeballs is also centrally regulated. Without this, visual perception would be impossible. When looking at an object, the eyes make sweeping, searching movements. If the retina is stationary, there is no light perception; it has to be *shifted in relation to the object* surveyed for a visual sensation to come about. The movements of the eyeball have been photographed by Yarbus, as shown in Fig. 17. It has been proved by Pritchard that visual perception is impossible if the eyeball cannot be moved in relation to the stimulus. He mounted a microprojector on a contact lens and thus prevented the movement of the retina in relation to the pictures projected onto it by help of this apparatus. A clear picture was seen by the experimental subject in the first second of the experiment, but soon it became blurred, disappeared, and returned only partially (Fig. 18).

The three pairs of muscles serving the movement of the eyeball are in fact controlled by the occipital visual cortex, but they are also directly regulated by the "searching" cortex (Brodmann's area 8, a premotor zone of the frontal lobe), or rather by nuclei of the midbrain and medulla oblongata subordinated to area 8 (Fig. 19).

Searching movements of the eye

65

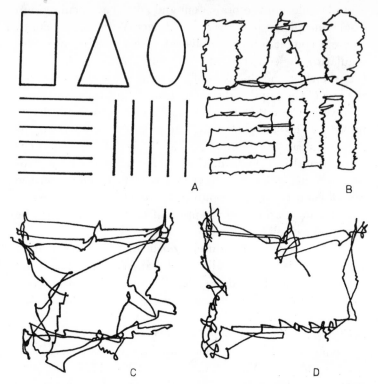

Fig. 17. Eye movements registered during examination of geometric figures. The figures in A can be examined in different ways. (B) The subject was instructed to examine the figures one by one. (C) and (D) The subject examined the figures without any special instruction being given.

Efferent control of the retina   Little is known about the third important mechanism of central control of visual perception. As has been mentioned, efferent fibers have been found to run from the brain to all sensory organs, which most probably serve to transmit impulses of central control. This efferent control of the retina has been described by Dodt as well as by Granit. A layer of what has been called *associative* neurons and *amacrine*

66

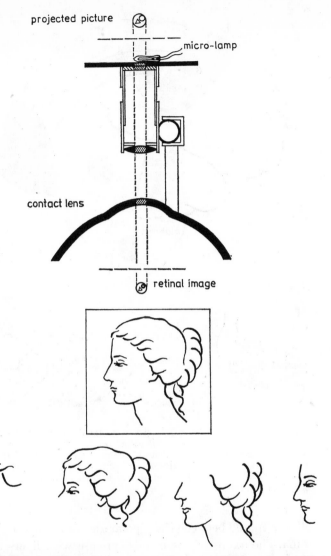

Fig. 18. Pritchard's projector mounted on a contact lens (top) with which he was able to project onto the retina figures which remained stationary in relation to the retina. The figure became partially or completely blurred within a few seconds (bottom). Acute vision is possible only if the light stimulus or the retina can make micromovements during the examination of the figure.

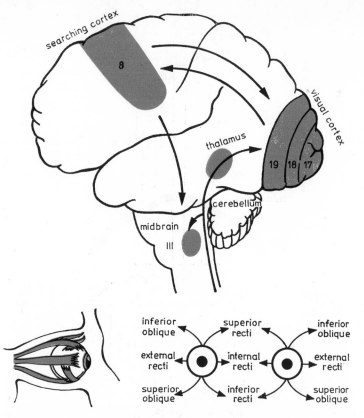

Fig. 19. Central control of visual searching movements. The searching cortex (area 8) is situated on the frontal lobe and is closely connected with the visual cortex (areas 17, 18, 19) of the occipital lobe. The three pairs of ocular muscles serving the movement of the eyeball are shown below.

cells is situated between the bipolar and ganglion cells of the retina. The axons of these cells synapse with fibers terminating in unidentified areas in the central nervous system, most probably in the reticular system (see below). The receptor impulses evoked by the light stimulus can be modified by stimulating these fibers.

The perception of patterns

If the inner, illuminated surface of a hemispherical object, e.g., a ping-pong ball, is placed immediately before the eye of an experimental subject, only a minimal amount of light will be perceived without any specific visual sensation (*Ganzfeld* experiment). This absence of perceptual experience is independent of the color and illumination of the homogeneous field and is related with the lack of a *minimum articulation*. For visual perception to come about the object viewed must show some kind of organization and *structure* (this, of course, in addition to the above-mentioned movements, which are also indispensable prerequisites of visual function). Lack of articulation will sooner or later lead to hallucinations, as for example in the case of the phenomenon of mirages sometimes experienced in lowland plains where the uniformity of landscape and sky causes hallucinations.

Perception of pattern is a congenital ability because the above-described retinal, thalamic, and cortical mechanisms **Perception of pattern** processing visual information are functioning from the moment of birth. Nevertheless, there are also very important *learned* elements involved in form perception. It has been shown that children under the age of six are unable to recognize puzzle pictures or concealed figures or to separate superimposed photographs. This is due to their limited ability of form perception. Children take a longer time to recognize complex figures but, at the same time, grasp figures which are upside down more easily. This is understandable because the reduced inverted image on the retina is turned upright again in the brain, a function which is labile in children and is stabilized in the course of maturation. Under the age of six tunnel vision is present, i.e., figures situated peripherally in the visual field are not perceived. The attention of even babies is much more easily attracted by figures of familiar objects than by unfamiliar pictures (Fig. 20). All these findings indicate the role of experience and learning in pattern perception. If congenital cataracts are removed from the eyes, it takes months until the previous tactile sensations are identified with the new visual experiences, and the function of pattern perception develops only gradually. Colors are distinguished by these patients sooner than shapes. In the beginning they may be unable to distinguish a square from a hexagon, or the feathers of a cock from a horse's tail. Thus, the importance

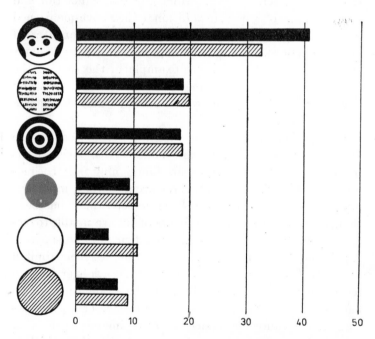

Fig. 20. The articulation of a figure is more important than its color or illumination in the perception by children. Even babies (black columns) fixate familiar figures like that of the human face for longer periods than figures of other organization. The same differences were also found with infants older than 3 months (shaded columns). The abscissa indicates the duration of fixation as a percentage of the total period of observation (after Fantz).

of learned factors in pattern perception is again demonstrated by these observations.

The function of pattern perception has been found to be present in invertebrates. For instance, the octopus is able to distinguish between different triangles, but cannot discriminate mirror images. Interestingly, it can distinguish better between horizontal and vertical lines, or between ⊔ and ⊓ shapes than between ⊏ and ⊐ shapes. There are several invertebrate species which are able to recognize their masked lifeless victims (e.g., the jumping spiders). Insects, having compound eyes, are generally good pattern perceivers. The outstanding pattern- and color-perceiving abilities of bees were described long ago by Frisch. Almost all vertebrate species possess this quality. The excellent visual sense of direction of migratory birds is known to everyone. For instance, the warbler finds its way by the configuration of the stars at night, but may also be stimulated by exposing it to the projected spots of light representing the stars in a planetarium. The pattern perception of rats was described by Lashley, and that of monkeys by Klüver.

Visual perception of depth and distance

The distance of an object can be assessed by human subjects even if they look at it with only one eye. In the case of *monocular vision* the distance of various objects from the eye, i.e., the third dimension, is inferred from various cues such as the relative size of objects and their illumination and interposition. This ability is acquired in early childhood by means of conditioned reflexes.

In an experiment the cage of newly hatched chicks, which have monocular vision, was illuminated from below after grain had been spread over the bottom of the cage. A few days later the chicks were shown photographs of cages; they started pecking at those pictures which showed the cage illuminated from below. This shows that learning makes it possible to assess distance and depth even in the case of monocular vision.

Stereoscopic vision Depth perception is more perfect if there is *binocular vision*. In this case the images that the two eyes transmit to the visual cortex are slightly different. The closer the object looked at, the greater the disparity between the images. The fusion of the two images forms the basis of three-dimensional, i.e., *stereoscopic*, vision. The image of the right eye shows more of the right side of the object, and that of the left eye contains a larger part of that side, just like two photographs taken with two cameras at a small distance from each other. The two images are fused in the cortical visual center, producing the depth effect of binocular vision. This, in fact, is due to stimulation of nonidentical retinal points. Elements of the objects viewed which are projected onto nonidentical temporal retinal points will be seen standink out from the plane of the image, while those falling on nonidentical retinal points near the nose will be in the background. Elements falling on identical retinal points are seen in the same plane.

Two flat pictures can be combined by means of mirrors or prisms arranged to present images to the two eyes separately, so as to give the impression of three-dimensional vision. The instrument used for this purpose is called a stereoscope. If two identical pictures are looked at in this manner there will be no depth effect. The stereoscope has also been adapted for viewing faraway objects, the three-dimensional perception of which is impossible because of the great distance. In the telestereoscope thus obtained the disparity between the two eyes is increased by substituting large mirrors for the pictures of the stereoscope. The image of the object viewed is then reflected into the eye by another pair of mirrors.

If forged documents or counterfeit money produce a three-dimensional picture when placed in a stereoscope with the original, this proves the forgery by demonstrating that small differences in contour exist between the two.

Stereoscopic vision is a learned cortical function. The binocular images are fused in the cells of the cortex. Several neurons responding to the stimulation of both retinas have been found in the cortex by microelectrode studies, indicating that the impulses arriving from the two eyes *converge* in these cells. **Fusion**

The experimental data available on light perception are more numerous than those on all other sense organs taken together. In man, vision is the sense showing the highest organization; this is understandable even to the nonbiologist or nonpsychologist in view of the priority of vision among the different senses. Therefore, the other sensory systems will only be discussed in terms of their differences from the visual system.

Chapter 3

Perception of mechanical vibrations: hearing

According to Sherrington's classification the auditory apparatus belongs to the class of mechanoreceptors. It is a system specialized to receive mechanical vibrations between 16 and 20,000 Hz (hertz = cycles per second). The information processing of the auditory apparatus resembles that of the visual system in many ways.

Structure of the auditory analyzer

Popular bionic model   The human auditory apparatus is a highly sensitive receptor. Its structure has been thoroughly studied by researchers of a new discipline, bionics, who would like to construct an instrument of similar sensitivity and selectivity. The sensitivity of the human ear is a matter of common experience. The ear responds to extremely fine vibrations, almost equivalent in energy to the impact of the molecules of air hitting the tympanic membrane. At the same time, it resists the extremely strong vibrations generated by a pneumatic drill or supersonic aircraft. As a well-known example of selectivity we may cite the experience familiar to everyone that one can direct one's attention to the voice of a single speaker in a noisy room. Likewise, musicians are able to select and follow the tune played by a single instrument from among the clamor of an orchestra.

The peripheral receptor organ of audition, the organ of Corti, is situated in the inner ear. It receives the vibrations transmitted by the tympanic membrane and the ossicles of the middle ear, transforms them into electric impulses, and transmits them to the brain. The human ear is not sensitive to vibrations below 100 Hz, and therefore normally the sounds produced by the movements of one's own muscles, tendons, and other parts of the body are not heard. The highest frequencies, bordering on ultrasound, are only perceived by young people; the upper limit of the audible frequency range is gradually lowered after the age of 30, by as much as 100–120 Hz per year.

The sound waves set the tympanic membrane (ear drum) into vibration, which is then transmitted across the middle ear by three small bones (the hammer, anvil, and stirrup) to the fluid filling the inner ear. The innermost of the three bones, the stirrup (weighing about 1.2 mg), makes contact with the fluid of the inner ear through an oval window and, acting like a piston, sets the inner-ear liquid into motion in accordance with the rhythm of the sound waves. The vibration of the fluid, in turn, initiates the vibration of the membrane of the organ of Corti. This complicated system of transmission is, in fact, very efficient: vibrations of great amplitude and low energy are transformed into vibrations of much lower amplitude but 20-fold increased intensity. Sound waves are transmitted not only through the ear-drum; the bones of the skull are also able to conduct the vibrations. The tone of our own voice as we hear it is always different from that heard by others because the sound waves generated in the larynx and oral cavity are also trans-

Role of the middle ear

75

mitted into the inner ear through *bone transmission*. The sound heard thus results from *double*, i.e., middle ear and bone, transmission. Others hear the same sounds only by middle ear transmission, which is less sensitive to lower frequencies.

Organ of Corti The organ of Corti contains *hair cells* (Fig. 21), which when reached by the vibratory pressure transmitted into the inner ear induce receptor potentials. The vibrations of the inner-ear fluid pass to the basilar membrane situated in the cochlea, which is a snail-like structure, 33 mm long, with $2^3/_4$ whorls. *Low-frequency* vibrations are transmitted to the *apical* parts of the basilar membrane, while *high tones* are transmitted to the *base*. The deformed hair cells are thus mechanically stimulated and convert the analog signal of displacement into series of digital impulses.

Thalamic center Each of the hair cells is connected with the fibers of two neurons, which are bipolar nerve cells situated in ganglia close to the inner ear. These are the first neurons of the auditory pathway, which, in contrast to the visual pathway consisting of three neurons, is built up of five neurons (Fig. 22). Most of these fibers cross over in passing to the brain, but some do not. The thalamus is an important transmitting station, from the medial geniculate body of which the fifth neuron starts toward the auditory cortex.

Auditory cortex The auditory cortex has been accurately mapped using the method of evoked potentials. Multiple representation has been demonstrated at the upper margin of the temporal lobe, near the lower edge of the fissure of Sylvius. This means that the auditory impulses arriving from individual receptor cells in the organ of Corti activate several cortical neuron groups simultaneously. The cortical projection areas show the same somatotopical structure as the visual cortex, i. e., impulses induced by high tones are projected to points which are separate from those to which low tones are projected, consistent with the differences observed in the stimulation of different regions of the organ of Corti.

76

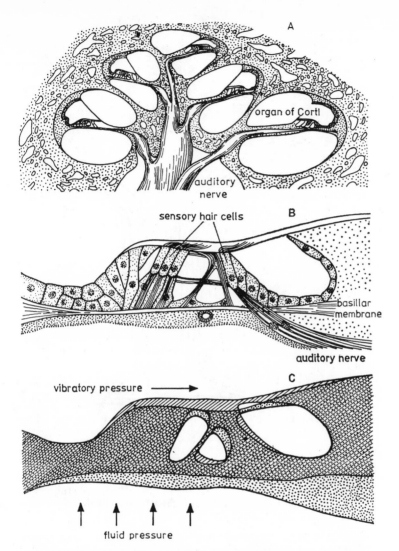

A

organ of Corti

auditory nerve

sensory hair cells   B

basillar membrane

auditory nerve

vibratory pressure →   C

fluid pressure

Fig. 21. The organ of Corti in the inner ear. (A) cross section of the cochlea with the hair cells. (B) structure of the organ of Corti. (C) Effect of vibratory pressure on the receptor cells. Arrows indicate the direction of pressure in the endolymph filling the inner ear (after Békésy).

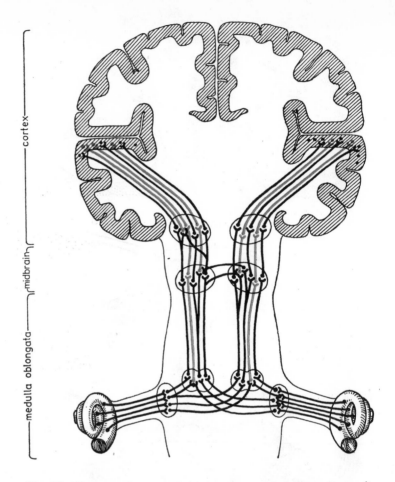

Fig. 22. Neurons of the auditory pathway. Red fibers transmit impulses from both ears. The number of fibers increases toward the cortex. The diagram is greatly simplified.

This so-called *tonotopical organization* is characteristic of the *entire* auditory pathway, i.e., of the cochlea, medial geniculate body, and auditory cortex.

78

Coding and decoding in the auditory system

The trains of action potentials generated in the bipolar neurons which are in contact with the cells in response to sound stimuli have been studied with the microelectrode method. There are cells which may also fire without stimu-

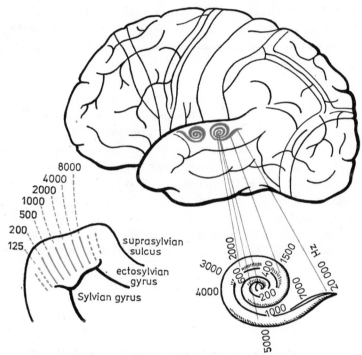

Fig. 23. Primary and secondary representation of the organ of Corti in the human cortex. Bottom left, topographic organization of the auditory cortex of the dog with representation of different frequencies.

lation (neurons with 10 Hz and 50 Hz frequency). Cells belonging to the other type are called "silent" because they only fire in response to sound stimuli.

Single sounds produce impulses within a circumscribed group of fibers of the auditory pathway; these are surrounded by "silent" fibers which are in an inhibited state. The phenomenon of contrast perception, i.e., the condition that stimulated groups of cells are surrounded by inhibited ones, which has been mentioned in connection with visual perception, may also be encountered in the auditory pathway. The perception of *pitch* (frequency) depends on the position of the stimulated fibers within the pathway, more precisely on their *borders* with neighboring fibers. *Intensity*, on the other hand, is dependent upon the *number* of fibers. Both parameters are probably important from the point of view of cerebral decoding.

Orientation in time and space

The tonotopic organization according to frequencies of the auditory cortex (Fig. 23) must be imagined as a *statistical* rather than a point-by-point representation. There may be considerable overlapping between neighboring areas, but at the same time such areas may show considerable differences in their frequency sensitivity. The columnlike organization of the cortex is also found here, just as in the visual cortex. Cortical areas lying vertically under neurons responding specifically to a certain frequency of sound all respond to the specific stimulus in the same manner.

Perception of acoustic configuration and direction of sounds

Decorticated cats were found to retain their ability to distinguish between stimuli of different pitch. This shows that frequency discrimination is a thalamic function; the cortex apparently has more complex functions. Impulses generated by stimuli arriving to the two ears are *fused* in the medial geniculate body and in the cortical cells, like visual impulses coming from the two eyes are fused in the visual cortex. The final auditory sensation is the result of the activity of neurons responding to specific frequencies as well as of higher units having a coordinating function similar to that of the "complex" cells of vision.

Again: fusion

By recording the activity of single cells with the micro-electrode method, neurons were demonstrated which did not fire in response to a specific frequency. Some cells responded to an increase in pitch ("up" neurons) and some to a decrease ("down" neurons). Whitfield and co-workers believe that the organization of the auditory cortex is similar to that of the visual cortex, although data support-ing this hypothesis are still sparce.

"Up" and "down" neurons

Experiments with animals that are able to perceive ultrasound are expected to provide an answer to problems related to the analysis of complex acoustic configurations. They might employ bats, in whose brain were found cells responding to a wide variety of tonal modulations.

Perception of the *direction* of sounds is possible because of binaural hearing. If sound stimuli of identical intensity reach the two ears *simultaneously*, a single fused auditory sensation will arise and the source is perceived to be in the median plane. If, however, the two stimuli differ in intensity or time, the source is felt closer to the ear which received the earlier or more intense stimulus ("lateralization"). Thus the perception of direction of sounds is a cerebral function, i.e., the result of the analysis of impulses arriving with intensity or time difference. The *movement of the head* and its correct orientation in relation to the source of sound have an important role in the exact localization of sounds.

Perception of direction

If the two ears are stimulated separately by clicks separated by a time difference smaller than 2 msec, a single (fused) click will be heard, but it will be localized to one side. If the time difference is greater, the two clicks will be heard separately. The smallest time interval causing lateralization is 0.03 msec.

The lowest level of binaural fusion is the medulla and midbrain. Decorticated cats are still capable of primitive auditory perception, and conditioned reflexes can be built upon stimuli in experiments using such animals. They cannot, however, discriminate finer acoustic differences such as the direction of sounds.

Intact cortical function is indispensable for auditory orientation in space.

Cerebral control in the auditory system

The central nervous system is not just a passive receiver of auditory stimuli, but has an active processing and analyzing function. The most conspicuous efferent activity is the *turning of the head* in the direction of the sound stimulus.

In addition, efferent fibers run to the *special striated muscles* adhering to the ossicles of the middle ear. These fibers serve the purpose of a central regulation of the responsiveness of the ossicles to vibration: contraction of the muscles damps the vibrations, while their relaxation increases the vibrations.

The receptor cells, too, stand under central regulation. Efferent fibers originating in the medulla oblongata are found in the *hair cells* of the organ of Corti, which may inhibit the cells' responsiveness and impulse transmission.

Chapter 4

Perception of the mechanics of body position

Having discussed the two most important sensory systems, let us briefly deal with *proprioception*, i.e., the sensory system supplying information about the position and movements of the body and of its various parts. It is common experience that the position and movements of the head, limbs, and body in general are perceived without the control of the visual system. One is informed about the outstretched or bent position of one's limbs, about one's head facing forward or backward, and about one's upright posture even with one's eyes shut. The receptors of this sensory system are situated in the muscles and joint capsules, and in the vestibular apparatus of the inner ear. The name given to these receptors, *proprioceptors*, indicates that they inform us about the state of our own body (Latin *proprius* = own). Receptors in the skin, to be discussed later, also participate in signaling changes in body position; it is difficult to separate the touch and pressure senses from perception of body position.

Not all elements of static and kinesthetic information (concerning position and movements of the body, respectively) reach the brain. Impulses generated in the proprioceptors may activate congenital automatisms resulting in reflex activity that is not under cortical regulation but is controlled by either the medulla or the midbrain, or may pass directly to the anterior horn cells of the spinal cord. Some of the movements connected with upright posture are automatic. Adjustment of the position of the body and head reaches consciousness with a certain delay or not at all. Thus some of the phenomena occurring in the proprioceptive analyzer system remain *unconscious*, similar to the information processing in the visceral sensory apparatus to be described later.

Structure and encoding activity of proprioceptors

Proprioceptors may be found in the skeletal musculature, joint capsules, and inner ear.

Muscle spindles and Golgi corpuscles Those contained by the muscles are enclosed in *spindles* of encapsulated muscle tissue, 3–4 cm long. The annulospiral receptors are coiled around the muscle fibers of the spindle. If the muscle is stretched, impulses from the receptors pass to the neurons in the sensory ganglion situated close to the spinal cord. Other, less important, receptors are also found in the muscle spindle. *Golgi corpuscles* are receptors in the tendons, at their junction with the muscle fibers. Impulses from these receptors arise when the muscles are stretched or contracted. The fibers of the Golgi corpuscles, too, run to the sensory ganglion situated close to the spinal cord. The stimulus threshold of the muscle spindles is much lower than that of the Golgi corpuscles of tendons. For stimulation of the latter, extreme stretching or contraction is required (Fig. 24). An impulse only arises in the sensitive annulospiral receptors in response to stretching of the muscle to which they are attached. The impulses,

84

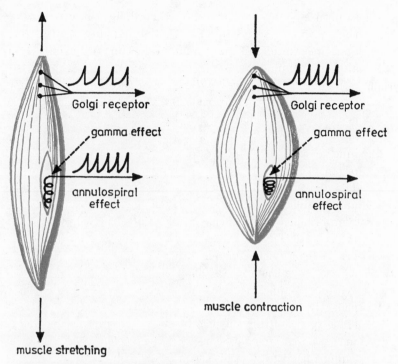

muscle stretching

Fig. 24. Scheme of impulse transmission by the proprioceptors. The annulospiral receptor only fires if the muscle is stretched, while the Golgi receptor, having a higher stimulus threshold, responds to both stretching and contraction. The gamma-efferent mechanism only controls the annulospiral receptors.

as a rule, take the shortest sensory pathway to the spinal cord, resulting in what is called the stretch reflex. The function of this system is to adjust and maintain the length of muscle fibers as required by the body position. The stimulus in this stretch reflex is gravity, in response to which the upright posture of the body is maintained. These reflexes are also called *antigravity spinal reflexes*. The impulses do not pass to the brain, and the reflexes remain intact in experimental animals deprived of all nervous structures higher than the spinal cord. The other pathway that proprioceptive impulses supplying important static and kinesthetic information may take runs to the cerebrum and cerebellum.

The labyrinth The labyrinth or *vestibular apparatus* of the inner ear is the other important proprioceptor. It is independent of the cochlea both structurally and genetically, although it is situated immediately above the auditory apparatus in the inner ear. The vestibular apparatus consists of the otolith organs (saccule and utricle) and the semicircular canals. There are three semicircular canals situated at right angles, and, similarly to the cochlea, they are filled with endolymph. The receptor cells, as in the organ of Corti, are hair cells embedded in a gelatinous mass (Fig. 25). Groups of hair cells are found in the ampullae of the semicircular canals as well as in the otolith organs. This means that each vestibular apparatus has five receptor systems. The hair cells of the saccule and utricle serve for perception of the static position of the head. Embedded in the gelatinous mass there are calcareous particles *(otoliths)* which are pulled on by gravity. The stimulus threshold of these receptors is very low, meaning that impulses are constantly passed on from this apparatus to the medulla. The nerve endings in the base of the hairs respond when the calcareous particles pull on the hairs. The receptors of the semicircular canals (hair cells in the *cristae*) perceive acceleration, either positive or negative, of head movements. Thus as long as the head is static, its position is signaled toward the center by the otolith organs, whereas its movements are reported by the receptors of the semicircular canals. The stimulus threshold of the semicircular canals responding to changes in the flow of fluid in the tubes is higher than that of the otolith organs. If the head does not move, or if it moves at a uniform speed, these receptors will not signal.

Not all the information transmitted by the vestibular apparatus reaches the cortex. Some only reaches the me-

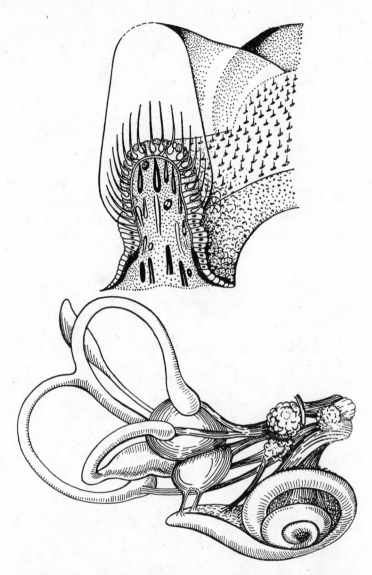

Fig. 25. The vestibular apparatus. Top, hair cells embedded in gelatinous mass. Bottom, semicircular canals with the ampullae containing the receptor cells. The labyrinth is situated next to the cochlea of the auditory receptor system; the two are, however, unrelated.

dulla or midbrain, setting off intricate but unconscious automatism regulating body position in these structures.

The projection areas of proprioceptors in the cortex have been studied with the evoked potential method. It has been found that although the major representation of proprioceptors is in the cerebellum, known to be an important center for the coordination of movements, groups of cells responding to the stimulation of different proprioceptors (in the muscle or vestibular apparatus) have also been found in the somatic sensory area of the cortex (Brodmann's areas 1, 2, and 3) (Fig. 26). Since the neurons of the sensory cortex are arranged according to the different parts of the body (representation of the head and upper trunk is

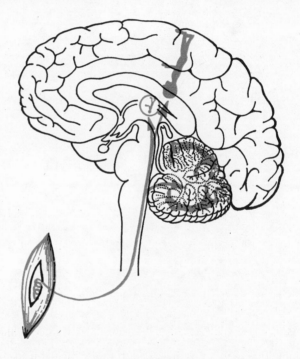

Fig. 26. Double representation of proprioceptors in the cortex and cerebellum (greatly simplified diagram).

88

found at the lower end, close to the fissure of Sylvius, while the feet are represented at the top), the representation of the different groups of muscles are also found in the respective areas of the sensory cortex. The vestibular apparatus is projected to the area representing the head. Similarly to visual and auditory impulses, those signaled by the proprioceptors also have a relay station in the thalamus. The thalamic nucleus ventralis posterior (VP) is an intermediate station for all skin, muscle, and visceral sensory pathways.

Proprioceptive impulses thus arrive on a complex self-stimulating circular pathway comprising the sensory and motor areas of the cortex, some neuron groups of the brainstem (called basal ganglia by anatomists), the above-mentioned neurons of the thalamus, and cerebellar structures. This reverberating unit regulating posture and the coordination of movements is known as the *extrapyramidal system* by neurologists. In contrast to the pyramidal tract starting from the motor cortex and passing to the motor neurons of the spinal cord, which is responsible for precise, planned, voluntary movements, and which consists of only two or three neurons, the extrapyramidal tract controls unconscious, coarse movements. The peripheral receptors supplying information to this system are the above-mentioned proprioceptors.

Cortical decoding of information on body position

It has been shown by Mountcastle and co-workers that the position and movements of the limbs are signaled to the brain by proprioceptors of the muscles, tendons, and joint capsules (Fig. 27). In experiments the peripheral train

89

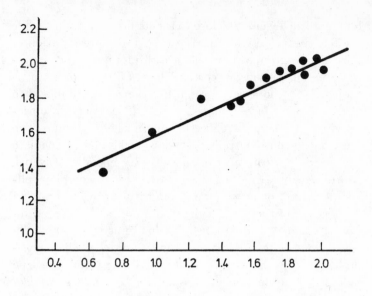

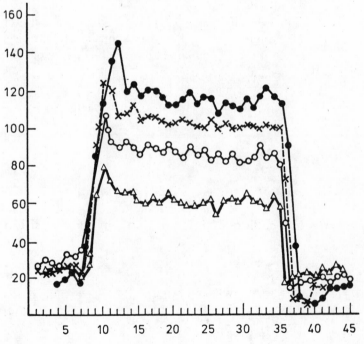

90

of impulses was followed. It was found that all sensory fibers participating in the regulation of motor activity of the limbs have a *stimulus threshold angle*. If the bending or extending of a joint reaches the threshold angle, impulses are transmitted toward the center. Some fibers produce "one-way" impulses, i.e., the maximum impulse frequency is obtained with maximal extension or bending of the limb. Other neurons, however, transmit "two-way" impulses; the maximum action potential frequency, in this case, is attained if the limb is in neutral position, and the frequency drops as a result of both extension or bending of the limb. Thus both the *angle* of the joint and the *direction* of the movement are signaled to the brain. Little is known of the impulse reaching the second neuron of the brainstem.

The data of Mountcastle on the decoding of impulses in the thalamus of the monkey are fascinating. The neurons are in general "one-way" structures, and their threshold angles are four times as large as those of the receptor fibers. For instance, if the maximum impulse frequency in a receptor arises at a joint angle of 10°, four such fibers converge on a single thalamus neuron which fires maximally at 40°. The frequency increases in response to bending in some cell groups, and decreases in others. The same kind of response to extension may be observed in other cell groups.

Fig. 27. Mountcastle's diagrams illustrating the connection between joint angle and the firing frequency of thalamic neurons. Top, frequency of firing of a single thalamic neuron (ordinate) in relation to the angle of continuous extension of the knee (abscissa). The larger the angle of extension, the higher is the firing frequency. Bottom, firing frequency (ordinate) of a single thalamic neuron at different fixed joint angles. Time is shown on the abscissa in seconds. Extension started in the 7th second and lasted until the 35th second. The firing frequency was the function of the joint angle.

The relation between the joint angle and impulse frequency has been expressed as

$$\psi = k \cdot \varphi^n$$

where ψ is the impulse frequency and φ the joint angle.

This exponential equation is the same as that given in Fechner's psychophysical law modified by Stevens (see p. 43). This is a good example of the identity of psychophysical and electrophysiological findings, i.e., of subjective sensation and objective impulse registration, indicating a linear transformation of cerebral events in the stimulus-sensation information system, from stimulus perception right to the verbal report.

Psychophysics and electrophysiology

The gamma-efferent mechanism: central control of muscle receptors

The gamma-efferent mechanism is perhaps the best known and most extensively studied example of the central control of receptor function. The fibers of this efferent pathway run to the muscle spindles directly from the spinal cord and carry impulses from the medulla and even higher centers. The efferent fibers are called *gamma fibers* because of their size ($A\gamma$ class of fibers). The neurons involved, similarly to the α neurons of the muscle effector nerves, are situated in the spinal cord. The function of this efferent mechanism is to adjust the contraction of the muscles of the spindles to the actual state of the skeletal muscles. The stimulus threshold of the annulospiral receptors is, as a rule, lowered by the impulses of the gamma-efferent fibers.

92

This mechanism has an important role in maintaining the upright posture of the body.

The gamma-efferent mechanism is part of a self-regulating system. If the body, or some part of it, assumes a certain position, the extension of the affected muscles is preceded by the arrival of the gamma-efferent impulse regulating the frequency of impulses arising from the annulospiral receptors. The contraction of the affected muscles is then achieved through the centrally directed motor nerves, the activity of which is, however, controlled in a reflex manner by the gamma-efferent activity. This system thus comprises an afferent and two efferent pathways (it is also called the *gamma loop*).

Chapter 5

Senses of indefinite classification: cutaneous and chemical receptors

Biologists, medical psychologists, and other specialists accustomed to think in terms of classical physiology, as well as laymen familiar with the function of sense organs, may be surprised by the above chapter title. It has long been accepted that the Meissner and Merkel corpuscles are receptors for pressure, the Krause end bulbs are receptors for cold, the Ruffini corpuscles are receptors for warmth, and the free nerve endings serve for the perception of pain. Recently, however, the specificity of these cutaneous sense organs has been challenged. Moreover, there is no uniform classification available for the chemoreceptors of taste and smell perception.

It seems most probable that, unlike visual and auditory perception, which consist of responses to well-defined homogeneous physical changes in the environment, the senses of taste and smell and the cutaneous senses are determined by combinations of stimuli of different modalities:

Physiological analysis of sensations arising from cutaneous receptors

If the skin surface is tested spot by spot, considerable differences in sensitivity to various stimuli will be found. The density of spots sensitive to touch, pressure, cold, or heat varies greatly in different skin regions. It is today believed that although the individual receptors of the skin display specific sensitivity to these stimulus qualities, the resultant sensations come about as a consequence of the combined functioning of the receptors. There is no heat sensation without tactile sensation, and vice versa. In case of extremely damaging stimuli, impulses arising from all these receptor types may contribute to the sensation of pain.

The pathway of fibers from the cutaneous end-organs to the central nervous system is well known. The impulses from the cutaneous receptors arrive at the sensory ganglion situated close to the spinal cord through the peripheral fibers of the bipolar (or pseudounipolar) neurons of the ganglion. The central fibers transmitting the impulses enter the spinal cord via the dorsal nerve roots of the individual segments. The pathway is similar to that described for the impulses of muscle receptors. Some of the impulses arriving at the spinal cord participate in reflex activity serving the defense against noxious cutaneous stimuli. The response is usually some movement of the affected limb, effected without the participation of higher nervous centers. Impulses arising from receptors of the soles, neck, of axial skin, together with the proprioceptive impulses, serve as sources of information for the mechanisms maintaining body posture.

The majority of impulses arising from cutaneous receptors reach the sensory cortex after double synaptic relay. The fibers carrying impulses from heat, pain, and

Pathways of cutaneous perception

95

touch receptors of individual cutaneous areas of the body are well delineated in the spinal cord. Similarly to the sensations arising from muscle receptors, the thalamic VP nucleus is a relay station for the cutaneous senses. Thereafter the impulses arrive at the Brodmann areas 1, 2, and 3 of the cortex, showing a strict topographic arrangement of projection (Fig. 28).

Organization in time and space   The coding of impulses generated by cutaneous touch and pressure stimuli (i.e., deformation of the skin) has been studied by Gray and co-workers with the help of the micro-electrode technique. The transmission of information depends on the *frequency* of impulses and the *number of fibers* conveying them. This means that temporal and spatial factors are equally involved in the organization of this sensory system. For example, the number of nerve fibers transmitting impulses from the Pacinian corpuscles of the sole of the cat depends on the intensity of the stimulus. It has been found that the parameters of mechanical stimuli affecting the skin can be assessed from (i) the number and arrangement of stimulated receptor units and of the attached fibers; (ii) the voltage and wave form of the resultant action potentials; and (iii) the distribution of stimulus threshold of the stimulated end-organ. It is conceivable that the digital signals arriving at the brain are decoded according to the same principle.

Stimulus intensity and impulse frequency   A strict correlation has been found by Mountcastle and co-workers between the intensity of stimuli and the frequency of impulses arising from the pressure-sensitive Iggo corpuscles of the cat's sole. The constant relation observed as early as 300 msec after the onset of stimulation has been expressed as

$$\psi = K \cdot \varphi^n + C$$

where ψ is the total number of impulses, φ the stimulus intensity (deformation of skin), C the frequency of spontaneous firing before stimulation, and K the correlation

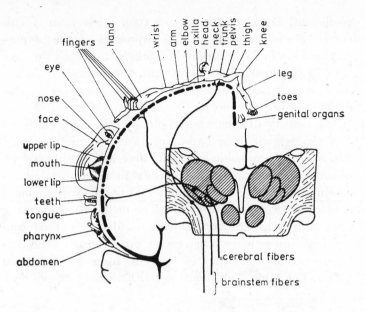

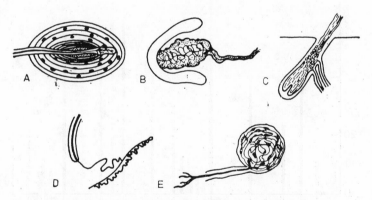

Fig. 28. Different mechanoreceptors of the skin (bottom, A to E)
and their representation in the thalamus and cortex (top).

coefficient. The exponent n, as a rule, is less than 1. This correlation is the same as that expressed by the psychophysical laws of Plateau and of Stevens. Just as we have seen in the case of muscle senses, the objective laws of impulse generation correspond to the subjective sensations examined by psychology.

Two-point threshold
The density of mechanoreceptors in the skin has been investigated with the two-point threshold method (Fig. 29). A pair of compasses is used for determining the smallest distance between two points on the skin which, if stimulated simultaneously, are discriminated by the experimental subject as two separate points. The distance between the two points is the smaller, the greater the density of the receptors in the investigated area, or the more sensitive the central decoding of the impulses arriving from the stimulated points. The same silent neurons (OFF elements) have been

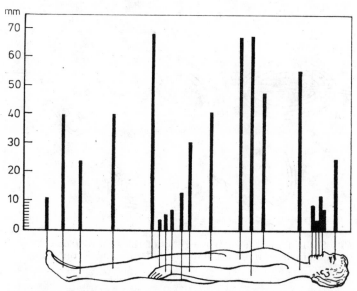

Fig. 29. Two-point threshold map. The ordinate shows the smallest distance (in millimeters) between two stimulated points permitting discrimination of the two.

found to surround the stimulated cells that have been described in the retina and organ of Corti. The discriminating capacity of central neurons has been statistically analyzed by Werner and Mountcastle with the help of stimulus-impulse matrices. The two-point discrimination mechanism in the central decoding apparatus is shown in Fig. 30, which reflects the results of neurophysiological investigations without making use of the inhibited (OFF) areas described by Mountcastle.

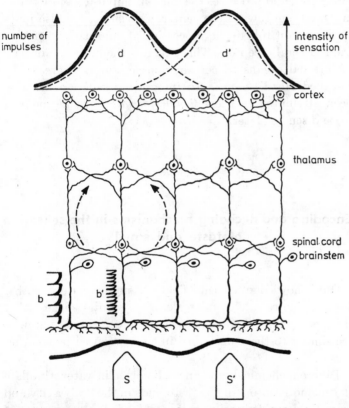

Fig. 30. Nervous mechanism participating in discrimination of the two-point threshold (according to Ruch). S and S' denote the stimulated points, b and b' the resultant impulses, and d and d' the two stimulated foci in the cortex.

Theory of pain sense The peripheral integration of pain sensation deserves special mention. It has been supposed that pain sensation in the brain (presumably in the thalamus) arises if the entire sensory system is stimulated by an amount of impulses exceeding a certain threshold. The sensory impulses are integrated by special apparatuses at the level of the spinal cord and medulla. *Rolando's gelatinous substance*, rich in neurons, found close to the site of entry of the dorsal nerve roots in the gray matter of the spinal cord receives, integrates, and processes the afferent impulses before transmitting them toward the center. This substance also plays an important role in the processing of information arriving from visceral receptors. This explains the radiation of pain of internal organs to certain muscle and skin areas, the so-called Head's zones. An integrating function has also been attributed to the *reticular formation* in the medulla to be discussed later.

Encoding and decoding mechanisms in the sensation of taste and smell

Our knowledge in this field is, unfortunately, rather scanty. The results of microelectrode studies suggest that the mechanisms of transmission and processing of impulses are similar to those described in connection with the other senses.

Taste Different chemical substances dissolved in water stimulate the chemoreceptors of the taste buds in the oral cavity and on the tongue. It is still unclear which is the component of the stimulating substances that upsets the resting potential, i.e., the equilibrium between the surfaces of the receptor

100

membrane, thus generating a receptor potential. For instance, if the four classic taste qualities (sweet, bitter, sour, and salty) are tested on a single receptor (e.g., on a salt-sensitive one), and the local receptor potential is registered

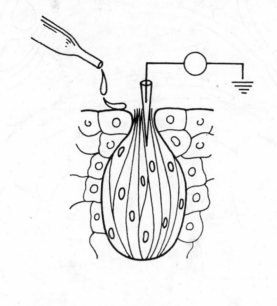

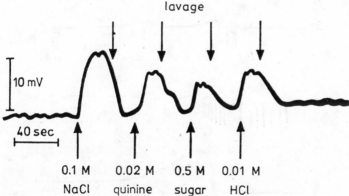

Fig. 31. Action potentials (bottom) from the receptors of the taste buds (top) of the oral cavity can be produced by stimulation with diverse test solutions.

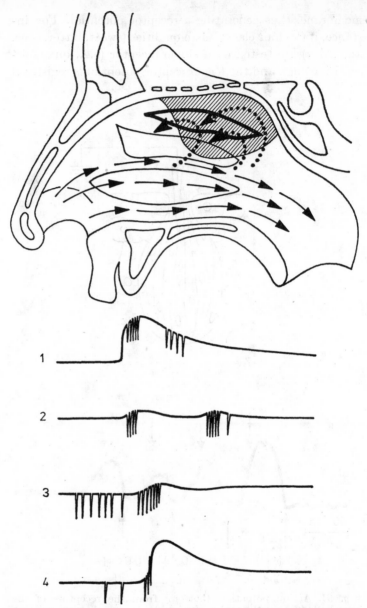

Fig. 32. The receptor zone (striated area) of the human nasal mucous membrane lies above the main air stream of respiration. To sense a smell a special sniffing activity is needed. Action potentials of different wave form may be recorded from olfactory receptors in response to the following stimuli: camphor (1), lemon (2), carbon sulfide (3), and ethyl butyrate (4).

by a microelectrode, potentials will be obtained not only upon application of salt (NaCl), but also as a response to the other stimuli (quinine for bitter, sugar for sweet, and hydrochloric acid for sour); however, the potentials produced by the latter stimuli will be weaker (Fig. 31). This finding has challenged the concept of the four primary tastes, the more so because normal tasting function is always a combined sensation, and the primary tastes are not perceived independently of one another.

Undoubtedly, the impulses transmitted represent a frequency code in this case, too. The fibers of the seventh (VII), ninth (IX), and eleventh (XI) cranial nerves carry the impulses to the medullary taste neurons and from there to the VP nucleus of the thalamus, which is, as has already been mentioned, an important relay station. The decoding apparatus is found in the mouth-tongue projection area of the sensory cortex.

Taste and smell are inseparable senses in human beings. **Smell** The *combined* deficiency of these two senses is a common finding in diseases of the oral and nasal cavities, e.g., in the common cold. According to some authors, under normal conditions we can hardly speak of independent taste and smell sensations. The receptors of the olfactory epithelium, situated high in the nasal cavity and having a total area of 2.5 cm², respond to the chemical stimuli of volatile substances (Fig. 32). No uniform classification of the smell qualities has yet been made, although a number of different systems have been suggested by different authors.

The elements of frequency coding are also to be found in the case of the sense of smell, but the impulses go straight to the smell center of the brain, the pyriform area, without entering the thalamus.

Chapter 6

Interoception —sensory function without perception

More than a hundred years ago Cyon and Ludwig published their work on the function of the depressor nerve originating in the aortic arch. Forty years later, in 1906, Sherrington, making use of additional knowledge gained on sensory function in the internal organs, incorporated interoceptors in the physiology of sense organs. It is a peculiar feature of this field that seventy years later interoception has still not been accepted fully as an integral part of the sensory apparatus. This is particularly striking, because in recent years there has been a constant flow of publications on the peripheral mechanism of receptors found in high numbers in the cardiovascular, gastrointestinal, urogenital, and respiratory systems. On the one hand, there are interesting data on interoception, while on the other, a synthesis is still lacking. What is the reason for this contradiction? In our opinion it should be sought in the overwhelmingly psychophysical interpretation of experimental findings, without trying to formulate a standard view on central regulation. In the psychophysical sense, sensory function is dependent on subjective sensation (which can be recorded by psychological methods) arising in response to stimulation of a receptor.

Contradiction between data on interoception and the psychophysical concept

It is beyond doubt that the experimental work based on the psychophysical principle constituted the basis of the important advance made at the end of the last and the beginning of the present century in the field of sensory physiology. The establishment of the relation between the physical characteristics of environmental stimuli and subjective sensation was of paramount importance in those days, and—as has been repeatedly stressed—the psychophysical approach is still useful in experimental work.

However, impulses originating, e.g., from the vascular walls or from the heart do not cause subjective sensation and thus cannot be assessed by psychophysical methods. This is why, at a time when sensory physiology developed enormously, the data available on visceral receptors were rather scanty. As early as in 1863 Sechenov spoke about "faint" sensations originating from the thoracic and abdominal cavities. Sherrington stated that interoceptive stimuli do not cause subjective sensations and, therefore, cannot be studied by psychophysical means. He attempted to demonstrate, making use of the methods of classical physiology, visceral afferent impulses causing changes in blood pressure in the cat. Although autonomic responses have often been used as objective signs of visceral afferent stimulation, reliable assessment of interoceptive function has only become possible in the wake of Adrian's development of the electrophysiological technique and Pavlov's conditioned reflex method.

The electrophysiological approach has yielded excellent results. For instance, Gray and his team did not only apply it to the study of cutaneous receptors, but also to that of an interoceptor, the Pacinian corpuscle of the mesentery of the cat. The quantitative correlation between generator potential and rhythmic firing was demonstrated in this interoceptive system. The basic characteristics of peripheral visceral receptors have been clarified in many respects. The same cannot be said of the central mechanisms of intero-

Electrophysiology and conditioned reflex

ception. Electrophysiological data are still scanty in this field, and information on the central decoding mechanism may only be obtained with the conditioned reflex method. Conditioning performed by associating the stimulation of

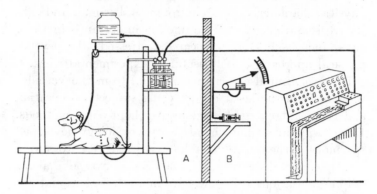

Fig. 33. Experimental equipment used for the study of interoceptive conditioned renal pelvic reflexes. (A) Animal in experimental chamber. A ureteral catheter had been introduced into the renal pelvis through a fistula. The renal pelvis was stimulated by introducing sterile boric acid solution at controlled pressure. EEG was monitored by help of chronic implanted silver electrodes and connections soldered into the dog's collar. (B) Observation room with syringe used for stimulation, manometer for controlling pressure, and the multichannel EEG apparatus.

visceral receptors with some unconditioned stimulus indicated that interoceptive stimuli do reach the higher nervous centers (Fig. 33). By this method the analyzer function of internal organs can adequately be studied. Bykov's interoceptive conditioned reflex studies have yielded important results, but this method in itself is not sufficient for elucidating the principles of interoceptive sensory integration. Complex investigations are therefore needed making use of electrophysiological techniques, the study of behavior, and also of introspection and psychophysical methods.

Structure of the visceral sensory apparatus

Observations of the anatomical and histological structure of the interoceptive system date back to a period some fifty years after the time when the basic physiological observations were made. The reason for this delay was that morphologists of great authority like Ramón y Cajal and others believed that all the peripheral autonomic nerve endings described in visceral organs only had efferent functions. This is understandable in view of the well established concept of Langley that the autonomic nervous system was of exclusively efferent character. In contrast, today the interoceptive system is looked upon as the afferent limb of the autonomic nervous system (Fig. 34).

Histologically the visceral receptors may be unencapsulated but circumscribed glomerular endings, or encapsulated structures. Their microscopic appearance, in contrast to their complex function, is relatively simple. Receptors of identical or similar structures may often be found in organs of different function, e.g., in the gastric wall and the alveoli of the lung. This might mean that morphological distinction of different kinds of interoceptors (e.g., mechano- and chemoreceptors) might not always be possible. The difference must be submicroscopic or chemical. Interoceptors are mostly diffuse structures, unlike visual and auditory receptors, which are parts of an organized apparatus. They rather resemble cutaneous receptors. A network of interoceptors may be found in all visceral organs, i.e., in the cardiovascular, gastrointestinal, and urogenital systems, in the different glands, etc.

Histology of interoceptors

The organization of the afferent pathways arising from these receptors is, however, much more complex. The majority of impulses arising from visceral receptors reach the central nervous system by four main tracts, the IXth and Xth cranial, the splanchnic, and the pelvic nerves.

Viscera sensory pathways and centers

107

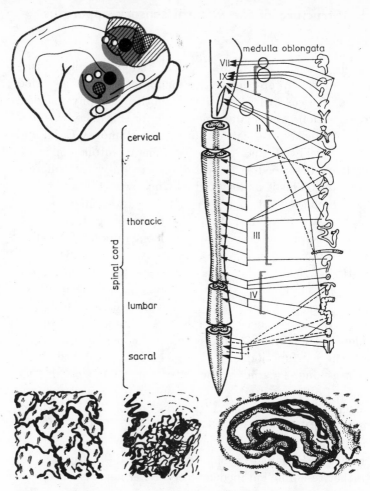

Fig. 34. Schematic representation of the structure of interoceptive system. Bottom, histological pictures of different visceral receptors. Middle, afferent sensory pathways from the viscera to the spinal cord and medulla, which constitute four main tracts (I to IV). The roman numbers in the medulla refer to the appropriate cranial nerves. Top, cat's brain with the representations of interoceptive afferent impulses (black, white, and hatched areas) and the two most important primary projection areas (in red).

The morphology of the spinal and medullary zones of entrance is relatively well known. As far as we know today the majority of afferent interoceptive impulses enter the VP nucleus of the thalamus, an important relay station which has been repeatedly referred to. The cortical representation of interoception may be found in the sensorimotor cortex as well as in the limbic area lying on the medial hidden surface of the cerebral hemispheres. This central representation explains the frequent observations that although interoceptive stimuli do not produce subjective sensations, they do influence human and animal behavior.

Encoding of interoceptive impulses

Visceral receptors in man are commonly classified into four groups: *mechanoreceptors, chemoreceptors, thermoreceptors,* and *osmoreceptors.* Lately a fifth type has been added, namely, *volume receptors.* Differentiation most probably is the result of phylogenesis. Future research may reveal other, different functional types of visceral receptors responding to different stimulus qualities.

Differentiation

Interoceptors of all types have two main functions: they constitute the afferent limb of special autonomic reflexes which have an important role in maintaining the homeostasis of the organism; and, by sending information about the state of the visceral organs, they influence the state of the central nervous system. Impulses arising from these receptors profoundly influence higher nervous activity.

Double function of interoceptors

The specificity of receptors to different physical energies has also been challenged in connection with interoceptors:

Paintal, for instance, demonstrated that mechanoreceptors of the stomach also responded to chemical stimuli. Further, Zotterman found that thermoreceptors of the tongue were sensitive to certain chemical stimuli. It has not been decided whether or not specificity is a characteristic of peripheral receptors. Some authors deny the specificity of interoceptors, similarly to that of cutaneous receptors.

Frequency code It seems proved that transmission of interoceptive impulses is by frequency coding, as has been described for other sensory systems. Some of the regularities of this kind of transmission were first demonstrated in an interoceptor, the Pacinian corpuscle of the mesentery of the cat. A correlation has been found between stimulus intensity (pressure on the carotid wall) and impulse frequency led off the sinus nerve.

Decoding of visceral impulses

Human experiments To investigate human visceral afferentation a thin duodenal tube with an attached rubber balloon was introduced, under fluoroscopic control, into the small intestine of an experimental subject. At the same time EEG records of the subject were monitored. The EEG changes ensuing upon inflation of the balloon, which by causing tension in the intestine stimulated the mechanoreceptors of the appropriate segment, were observed. Nonpainful tension of the intestinal wall was found to cause EEG desynchronization, i.e., blocking of the resting alpha rhythm (Fig. 35). Evoked potentials could also be obtained from specific cortical areas. At the same time, these painless stimuli did

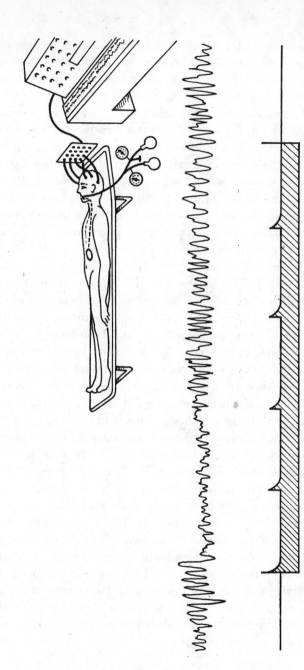

Fig. 35. Effect of nonpainful stretching of the duodenum on cerebral electric activity. Bottom, hatched block indicating duration of stimulation (time unit, 1 sec). Middle, EEG record, occipital lead. Note the blocking of alpha rhythm at onset of stimulation. Top, experimental arrangement.

not cause any subjective sensation at all—the experimental subject did not recognize the moment of duodenal stretching. This shows that interoceptive impulses do, in fact, reach the brain changing the electric activity of certain cortical neurons without reaching the sphere of psychic activities which, for lack of a better expression, might be called conscious. As has been noted, the impulses transmitted to the brain from visceral receptors do not cause subjective sensations in the psychological sense. Based on these and other observations, two types of afferent nervous mechanisms have been distinguished, namely, *conscious* and *unconscious* activities. Clarification of the differences between these mechanisms belongs to the future tasks of neurophysiological research, but discussion of the problem will follow in Part II. In connection with the visceral system we only wish to stress that, in our opinion, consciousness is the product of the social existence of man, developing in the course of active work. In terms of physiology this means that consciousness is entirely dependent upon the exteroceptive system responding to outward stimuli, because both social existence and work involve the analysis by the nervous system of information obtained from the environment. This is why it may be postulated that in man interoceptive impulses remain in the sphere of the unconscious. Still, exceptions to this rule are known, such as the sensory impulses arising from the urinary bladder and anus and perhaps also the visceral impulses participating in sensations of hunger and thirst. In the course of ontogenetic development man learns to perceive the stretching of the bladder wall and anus and to control the emptying of their contents. Presumably, the interoceptive impulses arising from these visceral areas are as unconscious after birth as other interoceptive afferent impulses. The child is then trained to perceive these signals as a result of conscious effort, to establish a conditioned reflex by means of associated stimuli.

Interoception and the unconscious

112

No data are available at present which would elucidate the cerebral decoding mechanism responsible for the unconscious integration of the enormous mass of visceral impulses and the conversion of unconscious pelvic visceral signals into conscious information. The study of these mechanisms is closely related to problems which will be discussed in Part II, those of conscious and unconscious activities, wakefulness, and sleep.

Part II

The energetics of mental processes: the waking state, sleep, attention, and consciousness

In Part I we discussed various aspects of the passing of sensory impulses from the receptors to the decoding apparatus of the cortex. Important processes were described at all levels of the afferent pathways, the aim of which is discrimination and selection of sensory input in order to achieve a favorable signal-to-noise ratio. In the brain the digitally coded signals are most probably retransformed into analog signals in the specialized receiving neurons arranged in accordance with a specific topography. The psychological term applied to this kind of converted information is *sensation*.

However, we have not discussed the second, alternate, pathway by which sensory input may travel. It is not enough for the sensory impulses generated in response to light, sound, or tactile stimuli to reach the specific central neurons of the thalamus or cortex for a sensation to come about. Conscious sensation will only arise if the central cells are in an *activated state*, .e., able to receive the train of impulses and to decode the information. To use an everyday term: the subject has to be awake.

The precondition of alert brain

The waking state, too, is the result of afferent impulses coming from the receptors, but these reach the cortex by *another pathway*. In the following we shall attempt to

Second sensory pathway

117

summarize the data that have become available in the past fifteen years about this special activating system of the brainstem. All nerves carrying sensory information, while passing through the brainstem send off *collaterals* into the medulla, midbrain, and diencephalon to a special nervous structure called the reticular formation, or reticular activating system. Fibers of this system run upward to the cortex, and through these fibers the reticular system is able to activate ("awaken") the cortex and to regulate its tone in response to sensory impulses. The fibers of the reticular activating system do not transmit information; however, no sensory information can give rise to conscious sensation without the mediation of the reticular system. In other **Dual pathway** words, the impulses have to pass through *both* pathways at the same time for a conscious sensation to come about. Until the brainstem is reached, the pathway is single, and it becomes single again in the cortex:

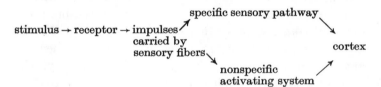

The recognition of the *dual pathway* of sensory impulses has been an important achievement from the point of view of neurocybernetic research as well. The reticular activating system is an important part of the self-regulating mechanism of central nervous structures maintaining wakefulness and attention and also participating in the determination of the conscious state of man.

Chapter 7

Alert neurons in the brain: waking and attention

Pavlov called attention to the fact that unexpected, **Orienting reflex**
sudden changes in an animal's environment result in corresponding changes in its behavior. For instance, in response to sound stimuli dogs show a startle reaction, turn
in the direction of the source of the sound, become alert,
etc. This simple congenital reflex was described by Pavlov
as early as 1910, and he called it the *orienting reflex*. He
emphasized that in experiments on animal behavior all
external disturbing effects interfering with the correct interpretation of the animal's responses to the stimuli under
investigation must be eliminated. Since all unexpected
stimuli elicit orienting reflexes, the experimental equipment
must ensure the elimination of such reactions. Therefore, **Pavlov's chamber**
he suggested the use of sound- and lightproof chambers.

Pavlov attributed great importance to the orienting
reflex, which, according to him, is an important basis of
animal behavior. His description of this reaction is the first
reference in the literature to the activating centers of the
brainstem.

Some 25 years after Pavlov's observations Bremer, a **"Isolated brain";**
prominent Belgian researcher, performed transections be- **isolated hemispheres**
tween the spinal cord and the medulla of dogs and cats and
observed that the reflex activity of these animals remained

119

intact and that the EEG indicated waking cerebral activity after this intervention. However, if the transection was done between the mesencephalon and the diencephalon, the animals were in the state of sleep and could not be aroused with any stimuli; their muscles were relaxed and the EEG showed the typical pattern of sleep. Bremer concluded that the waking state requires an intact midbrain and medulla. He called the animals with all cortical structures above the spinal cord intact "isolated brain" ("*encéphale isolé*") preparations, and those in whom the cerebral hemispheres had been severed from the medulla and mesencephalon "isolated hemispheres" ("*cerveau isolé*"). In these latter preparations arousal was unsuccessful. He reasoned that the isolated brain minus isolated hemispheres gave the cerebral center of arousal (Fig. 36) situated in the medulla and mesencephalon. This highly important discovery—as it has frequently happened in the history of

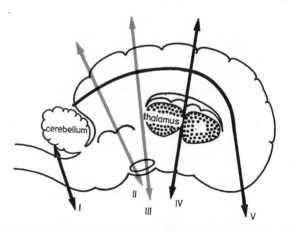

Fig. 36. Transections of the cat brain in neurophysiological experiments: (I) through the margin of spinal cord and medulla; (II) through the lower part of the mesencephalon; (III) between the mesencephalon and the diencephalon; (IV) before the thalamus; (V) decortication. Bremer applied sections II and III (in red).

biology—was soon forgotten, and was only recalled when Magoun and Moruzzi described the role of the brainstem reticular activating system in the 1950s.

The brainstem reticular activating system

The reticular network of nerve cells extending through the middle of the brainstem was described by the Hungarian anatomist József Lenhossék as early as 1855. Phylogenetically it is an ancient cell group, present in all vertebrates, which has a prominent role in the regulation of central nervous activity. In man the reticular system starts above the spinal cord in the medulla and extends to the diencephalon through the pons and mesencephalon. It is a particular feature of this formation that it is *laterally* surrounded by the sensory pathways described in Part I. Thus the fibers of the reticular system are situated centrally, surrounded with an outer coat of sensory pathways. The network of the reticular system is quite varied: the size of the neurons ranges from 10 to 100 μm and the arrangement of the cells is also variable. Slow and rapid impulse conduction is equally possible within the reticular system. According to most authors the system lacks all kinds of organization: no special structures are distinguishable within this diffuse elongated formation. Recently, however, researchers suggested the existence of separate cell groups within the reticular system. But it is still generally agreed that any distinctions that can be made within the reticular system are only functional: certain portions have been found to contain inhibitory and others activating nuclei.

Centrally: reticular cells; laterally: sensory pathways

121

It was first asserted by Cajal that all sensory pathways passing from the spinal cord and medulla to the cortex send *collaterals* to the reticular activating system. These collaterals are of prime importance from the point of view of reticular activation. In addition to these fibers, collaterals to the reticular system are also sent from the cortex, the thalamus, and the cerebellum. On the other hand, the reticular system also sends off fibers of its own to the cortex as well as to the motor neurons of the spinal cord.

The function of the reticular activating system was first demonstrated in experiments by Magoun and Moruzzi in 1949. They stimulated the reticular system through electrodes implanted into the brainstem and in this way produced an arousal reaction, i.e., waking the sleeping animal. By monitoring the animal's EEG, a corresponding transition from alpha to beta activity could be observed. The behavior of the animal also changed accordingly.

It is an important observation that arousal can be produced by the isolated stimulation of the reticular system even if the sensory pathways have been cut. On the other hand, if the opposite procedure is performed, i.e., if all sensory pathways are left intact and a lesion is inflicted on the reticular system with high-frequency electric current, the animal cannot be aroused from a state of deep sleep with any kind of stimulation. The discovery of Magoun and Moruzzi was found to correlate with Bremer's above-described observation and with the Pavlovian orienting reflex. The brainstem system maintaining the tone of the cerebral cortex has been called the *ascending activating system* by Magoun (Fig. 37).

The degree of reticular activity is exclusively determined by the impulses arriving at the system through collaterals of the sensory pathways, i.e., by external stimuli. The reticular system has no spontaneous activity of its own. Its function is to "awaken" the entire mass of neurons of both cerebral hemispheres. Maintenance of the *sustained*

122

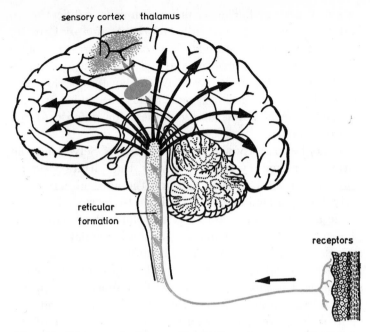

Fig. 37. Scheme of the specific (red) and nonspecific (black sensory systems.

waking state is probably a cortical function; the reticular system only "turns on" these neurons. It is a general alarm system responding in the same way to all sensory impulses irrespective of whether they have come from auditory, visual, or dermal receptors. Its function is to arouse the cortex and not to transmit information.

Most probably, the reticular activating system is involved in the regulation of endocrine function as well. For instance, if epinephrine is given to experimental animals, reticular activation may be experienced in the form of EEG desynchronization. It has been shown that epinephrine, i.e., increased sympathetic activity, invariably elicits reticular activation. This, in turn, enhances the alert-

Starting of the alarm reaction

123

ness of the animal. The resulting complex modification in bodily functions has been called *alarm reaction* by Cannon. Phenomena of this state are increased heart and pulse rates, a rise in blood pressure and body temperature, hyperglycemia, etc. The reticular activating system is thus also responsible for increasing sympathetic tone which in turn enhances the alertness and readiness for defense of the entire organism.

It has become known since the work of Selye that the entire hormonal system—primarily the pituitary gland found at the base of the skull and the adrenal cortex—is activated by a chain reaction initiated by increased sympathetic activity. Most probably, therefore, the entire complex system of defense and adaptation is regulated by the reticular activating system. Harmful external stimuli (stressor effects) activate the reticular system and thereby also the cortex through collaterals of the sensory pathways. At the same time sympathetic activity is increased and epinephrine is released prolonging the waking state of the cortex. The nonspecific hormonal defense mechanism described by Cannon and Selye as well as the reticular activating system are thus functionally interrelated.

Besides participating in hormonal regulation, the reticular activating system has other capabilities as well. Its involvement in the control of *motor activity* and maintenance of muscle tone has been studied in detail. Similarly to the sensory neurons of the cortex, there are a number of specific motor centers in the cortex, and subcortical areas forming part of the intricate self-regulating motor system that ranges from the spinal cord to the cortex. The cerebellum also plays an important role in this system. The lowest, spinal level of the efferent motor system stands under the control of the reticular activating system. This control is exercised by two kinds of effects.

First, reflexes regulating *body position* in the face of gravity and other external deviating forces, which we have described in connection with the proprioceptors forming the afferent limb of the cortical control of motor activity, are influenced by the reticular activating system. Their control is probably maintained through the *gamma-efferent fibers* running to the muscle spindles. Second, reticular influences play an important part in the maintenance of the resting muscle tone. Skeletal muscles are not relaxed even if they are inactive, but show a certain general tone. This may be compared to the strings of a piano, which are stretched before producing a sound. The afferent activity of proprioceptors (muscle spindles) plays a prominent role in the regulation of muscle tone (see p. 84). Thus in reactions of defense or aggression the reticular system not only activates the cortex and triggers hormonal reactions, it also brings the skeletal muscles into a state of readiness.

Regulation of autonomic function

The above-described functions alone establish the importance of this relatively small group of neurons, but it has been found that in addition the medulla is the center of regulation of all vital functions: neurons controlling respiration and nuclei regulating circulation and various digestive mechanisms all have connections in the reticular system. Neurons regulating autonomic nervous functions are also to be found here. It may thus be stated that this diffuse reticular system integrates all brainstem-regulated autonomic activities.

Inhibitory effects

It has been stressed that stimuli generating impulses in both exteroceptors and interoceptors activate the reticular system, which in turn increases cortical activity. There are, however, afferent impulses which, on the contrary, decrease reticular activity and thereby lower the tone of the cortex. Analysis of the fibers of the IXth and Xth cranial nerves has shown the existence of sensory fibers originating in the wall of the aorta and carotid artery, the stimulation of which resulted in decreased reticular activity.

The physiological function of these inhibitory effects is not fully known. They may form part of the *inhibitory*

125

apparatus responsible for the sleeping state described by Moruzzi and others. Reticular inhibitory neurons may be found both in and outside the reticular system. This problem will be discussed in detail in the chapter dealing with nervous phenomena accompanying sleep. Here the inhibitory mechanisms are only mentioned as part of the self-regulating apparatus of the reticular system.

Self-regulation

The animal and human organism may be regarded as an automatic system in view of its capability of self-regulation. Regulation in such a system is the process whereby the constancy of certain characteristics is maintained. The concept of regulation had been discovered in biology long before the era of cybernetics and computers. In fact, various biological systems have been used as models for devising automatic control equipment. The principle of *homeostasis* has been described by Cannon and has served as the basis of different machines devised for the study of self-regulation.

Feedback

Feedback is the basic mechanism of self-regulation, ensuring a constant flow of information into the control center about the effects of its commands. The aim of feedback is the adjustment of control and the correction of responses by the central regulating apparatus. In the physical sciences such a feedback function is called a *servomechanism*. Automatic control is impossible without feedback, i.e., without the control center being informed about the effect of its commands. Feedback is positive if it results in increased activity and negative if it has an inhibitory effect. Both types of feedback mechanisms are encountered in the sensory and arousal functions.

Cerebral control center

The most important part of all self-regulating automatic systems is the apparatus controlling adaptation and ensuring the constancy of its parameters. This part is called the *control center*. The human brain may be regarded as such a control center with feedback mechanisms modifying the commands to ensure optimal function.

126

If the reticular system is regarded as a control unit regulating the alertness of the organism, there must be a feedback mechanism inhibiting its awakening function. Several such mechanisms have recently been described.

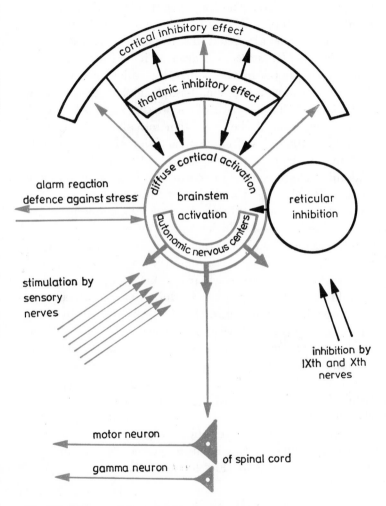

Fig. 38. Scheme of the complex function of the reticular activating system.

The first of these is the inhibitory effect of the cortex. The reticular system has in addition to its ascending fibers also descending ones which carry impulses from the cortex to the reticular system. Thus the reticular impulses which regulate the tone of the cortex are themselves controlled by cortical centers. The two together constitute a self-regulating system built on the reflex ring principle.

The thalamus also contains a nerve net, called the *thalamic reticular system* because of its diffuse structure, which participates in the control of reticular activation. As will be shown, the small-amplitude, high-frequency EEG pattern characteristic of the waking state is the result of the excitation of the brainstem reticular system, while the high-voltage, low-frequency activity of sleep is due to thalamic reticular activity (see p. 131). The reticular thalamic cells are antagonists of the brainstem reticular system. By electric stimulation of these thalamic neurons an inhibitory effect can be produced which is, among others, responsible for the slow synchronized activity of the cortex. The thalamic inhibitory structures were first described by the Swiss physiologist Hess some thirty years ago.

The activity of the reticular system is also antagonized by inhibitory neurons of the medulla oblongata described by Moruzzi. These neurons, though being integral parts of the reticular system, have an inhibitory and not an activating function. According to Moruzzi and others, the medullary inhibitory neurons play a prominent role in sleep.

The waking state of the brain is maintained by a self-regulating system consisting of the reticular formation and the inhibitory structures described above. The level of cortical tone, i.e., the excitability of the brain by sensory inputs, depends on the balance between activating and inhibitory mechanisms (Fig. 38).

Electroencephalography

Objective registration of the waking state of the brain by the electroencephalographic technique belongs to the routine tasks of neurobiological research and clinical neurology today (Fig. 39). (For a description of its discovery, cf. p. 36)

The chief wave type in normal human adults is the *alpha* wave, which is a regular sinusoidal curve. This activity was first described by Berger. The frequency of the alpha rhythm is 8–13 Hz. It can be best recorded from the occipital leads, and is the characteristic pattern in both physically and mentally relaxed subjects resting with closed eyes. **Alpha wave**

The wave form characteristic of active sensory activity is the *beta* rhythm. It has an average frequency of 13–30 Hz and a voltage that is lower than that of the alpha wave, i.e., **Beta wave**

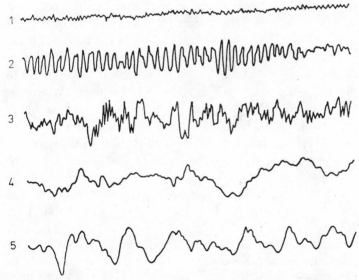

Fig. 39. The basic EEG waves: (1) Beta wave; (2) alpha wave; (3) alpha + theta wave; (4) theta + delta wave; (5) delta wave.

ranging from 5 to 50 μV. The beta wave is produced by different external stimuli (e.g., opening of the palpebrae, fixing the eye, acoustic or cutaneous stimuli, or other effects requiring alertness). Beta rhythm is registered from frontal leads in the resting state.

Delta wave The main wave form of sleep is the *delta* wave. Its frequency is 4 Hz and its amplitude is generally over 50 μV. It is registered in normal children under the age of 10 years in the waking state and during sleep in adults.

Theta wave *Theta* waves are transitory between alpha and delta waves, having an amplitude that is lower than that of the latter and higher than that of the former. It is normally registered in adults in the drowsy state before awakening or when falling asleep.

The above wave types may show great individual variations even if recorded under identical conditions. Nevertheless, some general conclusions may be drawn.

The high-amplitude delta and the high-frequency beta rhythm are the dominant waves after birth. The adult pattern develops after sexual maturation. Frequency is always lower, and the voltage higher, in the occipital leads than in the frontal leads. The electrical activity of the two hemispheres is approximately the same if recordings are made from corresponding sites. The frequency decreases (high voltage, low frequency) in response to low blood oxygen level or elevation in the blood CO_2 level, and increases when blood oxygen is high or blood CO_2 low.

The most conspicuous correlation has been found to exist between the EEG wave form and the tone of the cerebral hemispheres. The amplitude is indirectly and the frequency directly related to the alertness of the subject. Rapid activity is a characteristic of the waking brain. A transition from alpha to beta activity is observed if a bright flash of light is presented to the subject, or if he is told to concentrate on a mental task (e.g., to do a sum). This phenomenon is called *alpha blockade* or *desynchronization*.

On the other hand, the larger the cerebral area which is under inhibitory effect, i.e., in the state of sleep, the higher the amplitude and the lower the frequency of the waves. "Slow activity" is a characteristic of the brain which is not exposed to external stimuli. Since the EEG pattern gives a fairly true picture about the waking or sleeping state of the brain, it is made use of in surgical anesthesia.

If the EEG pattern contradicts the actual functional state of the subject (e.g., delta waves appear in the record of alert patients), this must be considered a pathological sign. Clinical application of the EEG is useful in the diagnosis of cerebral tumors, abscesses, epileptic foci, etc. **Clinical application**

Undoubtedly, the potential recorded by the electro-encephalograph is the sum of the electric activity of a large number of cortical neurons. The problem is, what kinds of *action potentials* are summed and what is the *control mechanism* responsible for the regularity of the alpha rhythm? The first question may be answered by microelectrode studies. Probably the spike potentials of cortical neurons are summed in some way and the local postsynaptic potentials are also involved. **Origin of EEG waves**

As regards the mechanism controlling the arrangement of the potentials into the characteristic regular wave form, we can only rely on hypotheses. For one thing, the regularity of the "slow activity" (alpha and delta rhythms) indicates that the groups of neurons in the area from which the potentials are led off are depolarized *synchronously* for some reason.

Synchronization is probably controlled by the thalamus. If the reticular cells of the thalamus are stimulated by series of electric pulses of 5–15 Hz frequency, a wave pattern can be recorded from the cortex which resembles synchronized EEG waves. It is presumed that the thalamic nuclei are responsible for these "recruiting" impulses. When stimulating the nonspecific thalamic nuclei, the recruiting-type synchronized waves appear all over the cortex. Thus it **Synchronization** seems that the synchronized brain waves of the relaxed cortex are controlled by the thalamic reticular system.

Desynchronization   The mechanism of the "rapid activity" is better known. It involves no synchronized activity of cortical neurons, on the contrary, a desynchronization of their firing occurs. It was observed soon after the first clinical application of the EEG that environmental stimuli lead to a disruption of the alpha rhythm, which then goes over into low-amplitude high-frequency beta activity. The finding that desynchronization could be produced in experimental animals by electrical stimulation of the brainstem reticular system helped to clarify how alpha rhythm is blocked by sensory impulses. This means that the intact state of the reticular system is indispensable for the waking state of the cortex, i.e., for the appearance of beta waves. The impulses transmitted through the specific afferent pathways cannot wake the brain without the cooperation of the reticular system. All these data suggest that the EEG pattern observed in awakening human subjects, i.e., slow, synchronized delta activity being replaced by more rapid alpha and then by beta waves, is due to the reticular system gradually joining in.

Two sensory systems   As also shown by the EEG waves, the receptors of the sensory system are linked with the cortex by two kinds of afferent fibers.

One kind is nonspecific, and is involved in the waking reaction registered by the EEG. The specific sensory pathways send collaterals to the reticular neurons; these fibers terminate diffusely in the cortex after several neuronal relays. Stimulation of the sensory pathways thus produces reticular activation and acceleration of EEG activity.

The other sensory system is the one described in the preceding chapters; it is the system of the sensory pathways proper, consisting of three or more neurons each, with well-defined thalamic nuclei, a high degree of organization, and *circumscribed* cortical representation. It has already

132

been mentioned in describing the methods used for the examination of sensory function that specific afferent impulses are manifested at the respective cortical areas as evoked potentials. Thus to the two afferent systems correspond two types of electric responses that can be recorded from the cortex: specific sensory impulses elicit evoked potentials at appropriate areas in the cortex, followed by the appearance of beta wave over the *entire* cortex signifying reticular activation.

Attention and habituation

Attention is the special state or energetic level of man when being awake. According to several authors, it is the psychological term for Pavlov's orienting reflex. The animal turns its sense organs toward unexpected or biologically important stimuli (e.g., those requiring defense or attack) in order to ensure the optimum conditions of stimulus uptake. Occasionally the animal may approach the stimulus and may make searching movements toward it.

According to some workers, the aim of the orienting reflex is to select the given stimulus from among a complex of simultaneous stimuli. Others say—and we agree with this theory—that *stimulus selection* is a more complex process than orientation and is what psychologists call "attention". Orientation is a *general* response to a specific stimulus; attention is more than that: it is the selection of certain stimuli and repression of others while the excitation of some neurons increases, and that of others is inhibited. The number of cerebral neuron groups showing contrasting states of activity increases, producing a higher

Attention: stimulus selection

133

signal-to-noise ratio with the aim of increasing the amount of incoming information. The orienting reflex serves the same purpose, i.e., it increases the amount of information, but no special screening devices are employed; in other words, there is little inhibition. In attention, however, inhibitory mechanisms play an important role. A more detailed discussion of the problem will be given when we deal with learning.

From the point of view of neurophysiology, *orientation* is first of all a *reticular* function. The stimulus "switches on" the activating system of the brainstem, resulting in a diffuse arousal of the entire hemisphere. Attention is based on this nonspecific increase in cortical tone, but it is a *thalamic* and *cortical* function. The excitation of unnecessary foci is inhibited voluntarily or spontaneously. The evoked potentials of several dozen points of the cortex were recorded simultaneously by Livanov, who applied a multichannel apparatus for visualizing the cortical phenomena of attention in the form of bright and fading spots of light. On his electroencephaloscopic screen the "migration", i.e., spread and concentration of the foci of activity, could be followed.

"Attention" neurons
By the use of microelectrodes, special neurons called attention units have been found in the cortex. For instance, Galambos found such neurons in the auditory cortex. Action potentials from these cells could only be recorded if the behavior of the cat showed attention directed toward the applied stimulus.

Both orientation and attention are transient processes. If the stimulus is repeated several times, the intensity of the responses will gradually decline. The stimulus ceases to be a novelty and the activity of the reticular cells decreases. Thus the increased tone of the thalamic and cortical nuclei cannot be maintained. This is what we call *habituation* of the orientation and attention response. Habituation is not the same as the adaptation of peripheral receptors, which

Habituation and adaptation

134

is a well-known response to continuous or repeated stimuli based on the elevation of the stimulus threshold.

Habituation is a *central* process: repeated stimuli elicit a gradually decreasing reticular response as shown by brainstem electrical records. It is an example of the plasticity of the cortex, i.e., of its ability to respond differently to repeated stimuli. In this respect habituation resembles learning. Its mechanism is not known, but it is supposed that a self-regulating brainstem system is involved, which consists of the reticular formation and its antagonists, first of all the cortex, the hippocampus, and the limbic system (see later, p. 154).

The phenomena of orientation, attention, and habituation which are under reticular control are thought to play a major role in assessing the amount of incoming information and in the selection of signal from noise.

Chapter 8

The sleeping brain

When considering the different levels of wakefulness, by necessity we are confronted with the problem of sleep, a special state of unconsciousness that might be regarded as the negative reflection of orientation and attention. The alternation of sleep with wakefulness is the most characteristic example of the periodicity of vital functions. As will be seen in the following, a whole series of physiological problems have been solved in connection with the sleeping state. Nevertheless, a basic question is still unanswered: why do we have to spend one-third of our lives sleeping? By the time we reach the age of 60, we have slept 20 years, of which 15 years have been spent in deep dreamless sleep and 5 years dreaming vividly.

"Bodily" and "mental" sleep   Sleep is the resting state of the entire organism. According to Economo, both body and mind rest in sleeping. The level of activity of all organs and organ systems is set by the cortex. In sleep the behavior of man and animals is characteristic: they seek a quiet place, assume a comfortable posture, and try to exclude environmental stimuli as far as possible. The stimulus threshold of reflexes is elevated and muscle tone decreases. As far as autonomic functions are concerned, there is a shift from sympathetic to parasympathetic tone: the heart rate is slowed, the blood pressure is lowered, body temperature decreases, and breathing becomes less frequent.

In terms of the function of the reticular activating sys- **Passive sleep?**
tem, sleep may be considered a passive process operating when the waking function of this brainstem system is absent, i.e., does not send impulses to the cortex during certain periods of the day. Such a theory was first advanced by Bremer, who produced deep sleep in cats by decortication. This, however, fails to explain the ineffectiveness of auditory, tactile, and other stimuli during sleep, the periodicity of sleep, and a number of other questions.

We must, therefore, postulate the existence of an active **Hypnogenic cells**
"hypnogenic" function inducing sleep, which is able to inhibit brainstem reticular activation. It was the Swiss physiologist Hess, who first proposed a sleep center theory. He stimulated the lower part of the thalamus of cats with implanted electrodes and thus induced sleep. However, since the effect of the strong electric stimuli he applied could not have been limited to the area indicated by him, and the cats spend 60–70% of the day sleeping even without special stimulation, his findings are difficult to assess. Moruzzi's methods appear to be more exact: by inflicting lesions on certain areas, stimulating them, and observing the chemical sensitivity of cells using a histochemical technique, he found hypnogenic cell groups in the reticular formation. These neurons are situated along the midline of the medulla, contain serotonin, and their destruction leads to the loss of EEG delta activity. In some animals there may be a connection between cerebral serotonin content and sleep requirement.

Dreams

Three signs of dream

Recent research findings have not only facilitated the objective registration of phenomena connected with sleep, but have also shed light on the problem of dreams. In 1953 Aserinsky and Kleitman reported on a rapid *movement of the eyes* during dreaming, which could also be registered by electrodes attached to the skin around the ocular orbit. Later Dement and Kleitman found a connection between dreaming and the appearance of *rapid beta-like waves in EEG records* with dominant delta activity obtained during sleep (Fig. 40). A third important sign of dreaming was discovered by Jouvet in cats: in addition to rapid eye

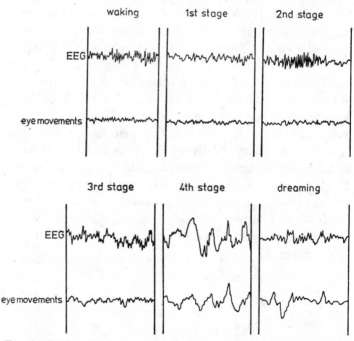

Fig. 40. EEG and eye movement records characteristic of different stages of sleep.

movements and EEG activity he observed a complete relaxation of the muscles of the animals. The retained muscle tone of dreamless sleep and this complete relaxation can also be observed in man. Sleep characterized by these signs (rapid eye movements, high-frequency EEG activity, and relaxation of muscles) is called "paradoxical," "deep," or "rapid-wave" sleep.

Jouvet also identified the cell group responsible for paradoxical sleep in the upper part of the medulla (in the pons). This darkly staining group of neurons in the locus ceruleus is inserted among the reticular cells and contains much norepinephrine and monoaminooxidase (MAO)—in contrast to the cells of "slow-wave" sleep (Fig. 41).

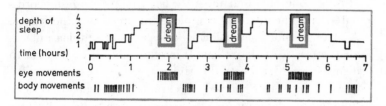

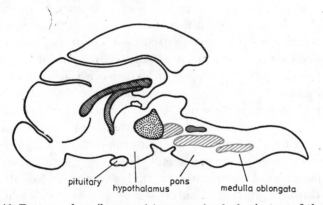

Fig. 41. Bottom, sleep (hypogenic) centers in the brainstem of the cat. Areas cross-hatched in red indicate nuclei connected with dreamless sleep, while the red area corresponds to neurons controlling paradoxical sleep. Top, rhythmic alternation of eye and body movements during 7 hours of sleep, including three phases of rapid eye movements (after Jouvet).

Thus both the dreamless slow-wave sleep and the rapid-wave sleep accompanied by dreams are regulated by lower brainstem structures, which are antagonists of the activating neurons of the midbrain reticular system (Fig. 42).

During a normal night's sleep the two forms alternate regularly: a dreaming period ensues after about 90 minutes of dreamless sleep. In most people three or four such dreaming periods lasting 10 to 30 minutes each are registered during a night's sleep of 7 to 8 hours.

The possibility of registering the outward signs of dreams, however, does not answer the questions relating to the essence and biological significance of dreaming. All we know is that dreams, which are often confused and bizarre, not always coherent, and mostly visual, consist of uncoordinated and uncontrolled complexes of previous experiences. A strong emotional coloring (pleasant or unpleasant) is characteristic of all dreams. It may, in fact, be no more than disintegrated intellectual activity.

Animals were deprived of paradoxical sleep by lesions inflicted on the appropriate centers in the pons or by preventing a decrease in muscle tone. The animals were subsequently restless even if they had had enough normal "slow wave" sleep. It seems that 60 to 90 minutes of paradoxical sleep each night is a biological requirement. Many animal species have been found to experience this kind of sleep, including the tortoise, various birds, and mammals— probably all vertebrates. It is not known of course whether they have dreams as well. Paradoxical sleep dominates after birth, slow-wave sleep only appearing after some days.

Does everyone
dream? The regular appearance of the above-mentioned signs of paradoxical sleep suggest that everybody has dreams. However, statistical surveys have shown that while some people can recollect their dreams, others cannot. The latter type may have the impressions of never dreaming. The ability to recollect dreams is connected with memory, a mental ability to be discussed later.

140

waking   dreamless   dreaming
sleep

eye movements

ECG

muscle tone

EEG

1 sec

Fig. 42. The three basic cerebral energetic states of the cat (after Jouvet).

Hypnosis

It is a long-standing experience that the depth of sleep may be different, i. e., it may be easier or more difficult to awaken a sleeping person. Different schools of psychology, neurophysiology, and psychiatry have proposed different staging systems for characterizing the depth of sleep. The criteria include consciousness or unconsciousness, self-control, etc.

Depth stages
Dement proposed four stages based on the EEG record: alpha, theta, and delta waves are intermittently registered in the first three, while in stage four, called the stage of deep sleep, delta activity dominates interrupted by periods of paradoxical sleep. The basic forms of sleep (slow and rapid) both belong to the fourth stage.

The other three stages of superficial sleep are of utmost importance to researchers, because in this fascinating condition between unconsciousness and consciousness hypnotic processes may take place.

Hypnotic state
For the physiologist sleep may be defined as a manifestation of cortical *inhibition*. This definition was proposed by Pavlov, who regarded sleep as an extension of inhibition over the cortex. In terms of this conception, sleep is the partial inhibition of the cerebral hemispheres. In subsequent chapters acquired inhibitory processes which interfere with learning will be described. Such local inhibitory processes which are limited to circumscribed areas of the brain may go over into sleep, and conversely, sleep may be reduced to local, acquired inhibition.

If a single stimulus causes excitation of a central area for a prolonged period, inhibition ensues; if the stimulus lasts even longer than that, the inhibitory process spreads to other areas of the cerebral hemispheres and the subject goes to sleep. Thus local inhibition and sleep are different

142

stages of the same process, and the former can be regarded as incomplete sleep. Thus, according to Pavlov, irradiation of inhibition is the essence of sleep.

For instance, if a conditioned reflex established to the sound of a buzzer is extinguished by presenting the sound stimulus alone, salivation will first be obtained to a few stimuli, but later on this conditioned reflex will disappear due to inhibition. If the sound stimulus is repeatedly presented in this stage, the muscle tone of the animal will decrease, its head will droop, and soon it will go to sleep. This effect of monotonous stimuli on man is well known; this is what happens during a tedious lecture when, due to inhibition in the auditory cortex, the words of the lecturer are no longer followed by the listener. If there is no new stimulus (e. g., an intermission), inhibition spreads to other parts of the cortex and members of the audience may fall asleep (this never happens during the intermission). Animals or human subjects easily fall asleep in an environment that is poor in stimuli (a quiet, dimly lit room), where the stimuli remain constant.

Normal physiological sleep is always an incomplete inhi- **Alert points** bition. There are always alert areas in the cortex which are in the state of excitation even during sleep. The depth of sleep depends on the size of the cerebral area inhibited. While drowsing we may still hear and see but may be unable to move due to inhibition of the motor centers. During normal sleep we make movements from time to time which are the result of the activity of alert points in the brain. The alert areas shrink to a very small size in deep anesthesia and in coma. Only the brainstem centers that have vital functions are still active in these states.

Numerous observations substantiate the existence of alert cerebral areas. Soldiers have been known to fall asleep on the march or in the saddle. This may be explained by alertness of the motor centers while other areas are being inhibited. The ability to wake up at a fixed time is also attributable to the activity of an alert point. Mothers have alert points responding to the stimulus of their children's voice. Other sound stimuli do not affect their deep sleep.

The transitory period between the wakeful state and sleep is called the *hypnotic state*. The nervous system is invariably in a hypnotic state when we fall asleep or wake up. Pavlov subdivided the hypnotic state into three phases, depending on the extension of inhibition and the corresponding reactivity of different cerebral centers. The first of these phases is called the *equilibrium phase*. There is no difference between the responses given to strong and weak stimuli during this period. For instance, the same amount of saliva has been found to be excreted in response to strong and weak conditioned sound stimuli. The *paradoxical phase* is characterized by deeper sleep. Weak stimuli evoke a more active response than strong ones during this phase. The *ultraparadoxical phase* means a still deeper sleep, when a response is only given to weak stimuli, and strong stimuli lead to more extensive inhibition. Deep sleep, in which inhibition affects the largest cerebral area, follows these three stages. It is a common experience that a whisper has a greater effect on a drowsing subject than a loud noise, and even whispers are ineffective once the subject has fallen asleep.

The hypnotic state between wakefulness and sleep has long been known. If an animal is kept forcibly in an awkward position for a longer period, the resultant strong proprioceptive excitation brings about a particular state: the animal falls asleep but its muscles are fixed in the awkward position. The state thus produced is a paradoxical hypnotic sleep (not to be confused with the paradoxical sleep of dreaming !). A hypnotic state is produced in man by exposure to monotonous stimuli, but care must be taken to keep points along the auditory pathway and in other cerebral areas alert by verbal stimuli to ensure continuance of contact with the operator.

Since Pavlov's work became known, hypnosis has been regarded as incomplete sleep by some investigators. According to this school of thought, a similar state is experienced, e.g., when sleeping sitting up in a train: one hears the conversation of the other passengers while they hear one's snores and observe other signs of sound sleep. This, indeed, is a paradoxical state.

The first mention of hypnosis was made in the book *Neurohypnologia* by Braid, published in 1846. Later Charcot, Bernheim, and others helped to clarify the connection between hypnosis and sleep. Pavlov's above-described theory clearly defined this connection. Hypnosis was welcomed as an important therapeutic measure because advice and commands given in the hypnotic state are more suggestive and their effect may be beneficial after the patient wakes up.

However, it has turned out that the problem is not all that simple. It has been found that the EEG waves in hypnosis resemble those in the waking state rather than the EEG of sleep. It has also been established that *some* people are more prone to being hypnotized than others, while there are some who are not responsive to hypnosis at all. Objective methods of assaying hypnotizability and of classifying individuals accordingly have been worked out by Hilgard, Orne, and others. The question has been raised whether people more responsive to hypnosis are more easily maintained in the state of superficial sleep. The answer is probably no. Consequently it may not be appropriate to consider the hypnotic state a form of sleep.

Indeed, in recent years hypotheses other than the sleep theory have been put forward. According to these, hypnosis cannot be equated either with sleep or with wakefulness, but rather is a special borderline state of consciousness which can be brought about more easily in one group of people than in others. This state has been compared to acting ability present in some but absent in others. It cannot be said at present whether the sleeping or the "acting" theory will eventually be proved.

Suggestion and hypnosis Hypnosis is thus characterized by enhanced suggestibility, but suggestion is not identical with hypnosis. According to Pavlov, it is due to strong excitation of a cerebral focus surrounded by extensive inhibited areas. Such a focus can also be brought about in the waking state under appropriate conditions. The emphatic advice or orders of the doctor given to his patient are, in fact, a kind of suggestion having a beneficial effect in the majority of cases. Autosuggestion, too, is a well-known mental process. It might also be called self-discipline, being an important feature of education even in young children. It is not known, however, why suggestion is more effective in the drowsy state (either the one occurring before falling asleep or hypnotic sleep induced by the specialist).

The fashionable idea of "learning during sleep" is connected with the above theories. An alert point may be established in the brain by training oneself to go to sleep while listening to a recorded language lesson (not too loud and not too quiet) and not to be wakened by the noise of the tape. In hypnotic sleep one may be able—quite unawares—to hear the repeated recordings. If the text is listened to in a conscious state next morning, it may appear familiar and may be learned more easily.

Hypnopedia Naturally, learning a language without conscious effort is inconceivable. At most, lexical knowledge may be acquired during sleep, but any learning that requires intellectual effort or logical thinking is impossible. The practice of hypnopedia raises a number of problems (the need for rest for people learning during sleep, difficulty of the adjustment of the adequate level of sleep, etc.), and cannot, therefore, be expected to gain widespread application.

146

Chapter 9

The conscious state and the unconscious

In previous chapters an often used but not well defined term has popped up time and again, namely, *consciousness*, a controversial notion which has not been explored from the biological point of view. It can, nevertheless, not be disregarded when dealing with the energetics of mental processes and with wakefulness.

It has repeatedly been mentioned that a number of sensory (visual, auditory, tactile) impulses arriving at the central nervous system are consciously perceived, while others, e.g., the interoceptive impulses, do not reach consciousness, i.e., do not give rise to subjective sensations. Undoubtedly, the empirical observation of conscious and unconscious impulses has directed attention to the existence of two kinds of nervous mechanisms.

Wakefulness is a physiological prerequisite of consciousness. As has been seen, the activity of higher centers increases in the wakeful state, while their stimulus threshold is lowered. The activating effect of the brainstem reticular formation contributes to this state.

At the same time, we cannot say that wakefulness is identical with consciousness. The absence of wakefulness precludes all kinds of perception or cognition, as, e.g., in sleep. But not all sensory processes reach consciousness even

Wakefulness and consciousness

in the wakeful state. We are aware of some (mostly exteroceptive) stimuli, but unaware of others (mostly interoceptive), although the latter have also been found to reach the
higher centers and to activate the reticular formation.
It appears that wakefulness is the precondition of consciousness, but does not account for it—as suggested by Penfield
in connection with the centrencephalon theory.

In terms of Pavlov's conditioned reflex theory, impulses
become conscious when assuming a secondary signal character, i.e., when gaining verbal expression. The stimuli of
the environment are not only perceived, but are also known
—as expressed by the Latin word *conscientia*. Thus, according to this theory, consciousness means the simultaneous
presence in the higher centers of impulses arising as a result
of primary environmental stimuli and those due to abstract, verbal signals. This is in agreement with an earlier
psychological concept defining consciousness as the sum
of all sensations and psychic phenomena at a given moment.
In this sense, the conscious state is the result of the synchronous activity of several cortical and subcortical functional units. It is also possible that these units are involved
in conscious activity as a single functional system.

The lack of a biological theory of consciousness
The number of theories relating the essence of consciousness is, indeed, formidable, and most of them lack sound
experimental foundations. No problem in brain research
has perhaps given rise to so many speculations as this one.
For instance, Kleitman, who did much valuable work to
find a biological interpretation of dreams, could only define
consciousness in poetic terms as "the ability of the individual to make use of the past and contribute to the future."
Moruzzi may be cited as another example. He defined the
physiological determinants of consciousness as an ability
to make use of sensory information, to critically respond to
this input with mental or motor activities, to trigger memory processes, and to store information.

No agreement has yet been reached by physiologists on

148

the definition of conscious and unconscious mental processes, although several scientific meetings have dealt with the problem. The volumes containing the proceedings of these conferences reflect the dilemma (cf. symposia held in the United States between 1950 and 1954—published in a volume edited by Abramson, and the discussions at the 1966 Moscow symposium in the volume edited by Banshchikov). Such uncertainties have been encountered in other fields as well when dealing with functional systems without knowing their biological bases.

A better approach to the problem is offered from the side of the *unconscious* as a result of data accumulating on physiological processes in the human brain which invariably remain unconscious.

Although philosophers of the seventeenth to nineteenth centuries, from Spinoza to Leibniz, repeatedly called attention to the importance of subconscious mental processes, it was Charcot and Janet, founders of modern psychiatry, who first applied exact experimental methods to the study of unconscious nervous activities in connection with pathological states of disturbed consciousness. Nevertheless, the problem of the conscious and unconscious came into the limelight only as a result of Freud's activity. His merit in calling the attention of psychiatrists and physiologists to this aspect of mental processes stands firm irrespective of whether we endorse his neuropsychiatric, psychological, or philosophical views. The scope of this book does not allow a detailed discussion of Freudianism or the different neo-Freudian theories. Freud's work, though much of it has been superseded, still has considerable effect on contemporary scientific thinking and should be seen in proper perspective.

The biological and Freudian unconscious

Freud maintained that man's behavior is determined, in addition to environmental and social factors and conscious processes, by processes taking place in a sphere of nervous activity which he—like some of his predecessors—called

Criticism of the Freudian unconscious

149

the unconscious. We do not challenge the existence of unconscious psychic processes but do not agree with Freud's further speculations. There is ample experimental evidence —furnished by neurophysiological research—that human behavior is indeed influenced by visceral proprioceptive impulses and humoral and hormonal effects. This information coming from internal organs is the source supplying impulses for the sphere of unconscious behavior.

Freud maintained that the individual is unable to adapt to his biological and social environment because of the unmanageable and uncontrollable unconscious, the inherited mysterious *id*, *"das Es,"* which consciousness is unable to govern. Consciousness and the unconscious in this theory represent opposite poles. Such ideas do not appeal to the neurophysiologist, not to speak about his interpretation of the unconscious in which complexes of the sexual and self-preservation instincts are given unduly great emphasis, his speculations about repression, abortion, and sleep, and the employment of absurd symbols and mythological analogies.

Freud distinguished the preconscious *(Vorbewusstsein)* from the unconscious *(Unbewusstsein)*. Elements of the former can easily become conscious, while those of the latter enter the conscious sphere only with difficulty or not at all. This argument is false. Psychological research has shown that with the widening of the scope of human cognition, the store of the unconscious also becomes richer. Elements of this stored material may emerge as required by actual mental tasks. The submerging of experiences into the unconscious ("forgetting") and their becoming conscious again at a later time ("recalling") are preconditions of normal psychic function. These opposing processes operate in unity and show a peculiar balance. Thus the unconscious acts as a *relief* and *reserve* force of the human mind.

The three pillars of Freudianism According to Freud, the unconscious has a content of sexual and self-preservation instincts which are immoral.

and irrepressible. The absurdity of this reasoning must be evident even to nonpsychologists. Man accepts and consciously applies instincts (and not only the two singled out by Freud) to build up a harmonious personality. The second main contention of the Freudian theory that unconscious instincts are the opposite of consciousness with all its rational, social, and moral implications is untenable. As has been said, these two spheres of the psyche are counterparts. The third main pillar of the Freudian theory appears similarly absurd to the scientist. He maintained that the basic processes of the human psyche, and mainly the unconscious ones, are formed in early childhood, and that there is little or no development in psychic life in later periods of life. This statement will be disproved later in this book when we deal with the plastic processes of learning and memory. It is common experience that both conscious and unconscious psychic processes maintain plasticity in the adult and even in old age, and the ability of cerebral neurons to store, process, and analyze information is preserved.

It is in the interpretation of the content of the unconscious that we disagree with Freud. From the point of view of the biologist, this cannot be restricted to a handful of—otherwise important—instincts. As a result of modern neurophysiological research, an ever increasing body of evidence is being accumulated on the emotional factors of human behavior, the connections between the hormonal system and brain function, the automatisms of motor function, and the so-called subsensory processes, including interoception, etc. No doubt, most of these are unconscious processes in man, even if not in the Freudian sense that instinctive behavior is a suppressed counterpart of rational behavior *ab ovo* restraining it. These physiological mechanisms, which have not yet been fully explored, are accessory to, or rather synergic with, the conscious socially determined or learned processes. In other cases they may, of course, be antagonistic. In agreement with other critics of Freud, we pay tribute to his ingenious empiricism and compelling phenomenology, but reject his theory on instinct, which is irreconcilable with the results of neurophysiology. It is his merit nevertheless that he directed attention to the problems of the unconscious even if his definition was false. Biologists of the Pavlovian school should attack this problem most emphatically, because notions of the conscious vs. unconscious are almost completely missing from the Pavlovian theory of higher nervous function. Without them, however, it would be impossible to deal with the problem of the biological aspects of the human mind.

Unconscious physiological processes

Automatisms

"Set"

Let us examine those cerebral processes which, according to psychological and psychiatric observations, do not reach consciousness. To these belong in the first place certain *forms of human activity* which are jointly called *automatisms*. Many of the routine movements of man are automatic, including gait and posture, and the same may be stated about one's manner of writing or way of speech. The basic vocabulary of the language and certain idiomatic expressions are used without conscious effort. These learned processes become automatisms in early childhood and later belong to the sphere of unconscious activity. Among locomotor automatisms Uznadze described the phenomenon of *set* (self-adjustment). For instance, two metal globes of the same size are placed before a subject. He lifts one which is heavy, say 10 kg. Then, based on his previous experience, he prepares to lift the other globe with the same muscle force. If the second globe, though of the same size, is much lighter, he will be "disappointed" because he has adjusted his muscles to lifting a much heavier weight. The set factor is part of human motor functions and is an example of learned unconscious mental processes in automatic forms of behavior.

A whole series of unconscious conditioned reflexes could be mentioned. It is known from the work of Bikov and his associates that visceral conditioned reflexes can be established by associating exteroceptive stimuli with autonomic reactions. For instance, if a human subject is placed into a room at a temperature of 30°C at the same hour of the day for several days, and his respiration, body temperature, and autonomic reactions are monitored, adaptation of the subject's thermoregulation and visceral processes to the higher temperature will be observed as early as during the second or third session. If, after a few days, the temperature of the room is lowered to 20°C, at first the subject will respond to stimuli in the same way he did in the hot room. This may be explained by the establishment of a thermoregulatory conditioned reflex to stimuli of that particular environment, i.e., the sight, smell, tactile stimuli, etc. of the room. Cardiovascular and respiratory function, the activity of the digestive glands (as shown by Pavlov in his classical experiments with dogs), the movements of the digestive tract, renal function, etc. may all be influenced by way of conditioned reflexes. This means that visceral processes can be affected by "neutral" environmental stimuli in an unconscious way via association with other stimuli.

Visceral conditioned reflexes

The *hormonal system* also belongs to the unconscious factors influencing human behavior. The level of different hormones in the blood circulation is known to influence mental activity considerably. The secretory activity of endocrine glands producing hormones ranging from sex hormones to those of the thyroid gland and pancreas is controlled by higher nervous centers. Through a feedback mechanism the

Hormonal influences

153

higher nervous activity is, in turn, controlled by qualitative and quantitative changes of these hormones. All these processes remain unconscious. Intensive research in this field has been conducted in Hungary by the team of Professor K. Lissák at the Department of Physiology, Pécs University Medical School.

Emotional reactions Emotional reactions are important subconscious psychic functions of man. It is common experience that human behavior is influenced, in addition to the above-discussed factors, also by processes which have been collectively called emotions or affectivity by psychologists. All external and internal stimuli have emotional qualities, e. g., they may be either pleasant or unpleasant. These emotional attributes also influence the response given to stimuli. The biology of emotions is one of the most intriguing problems of modern brain research. These, mostly unconscious, processes have lately been related to the *limbic region* of the **Limbic system** brain (Figs 43 and 44). The limbic system of the archicortex, found "hidden" at the interface of the two hemispheres in the medial zones, is closely connected with visceral functions (that is why the limbic system has been called the "visceral brain"), and also with emotional behavior. The animal experiments of Delgado helped to understand the function of the limbic system. With implanted chronic electrodes and two-way radio sets built into the collars of a group of monkeys, he telemetrically stimulated different parts of the limbic system. Depending on the individual disposition of the monkeys, on their position within the group, and on the site of the neurons stimulated, the behavioral response was either aggressive or friendly (Fig. 45). Thus the limbic system appeared to be connected with unconscious emotional behavior, but also with the relation of the individual to other members of the group. These experimental findings can only have limited relevance to human behavior since the latter is socially, and not biologically, determined in the first place. There is, however, an

154

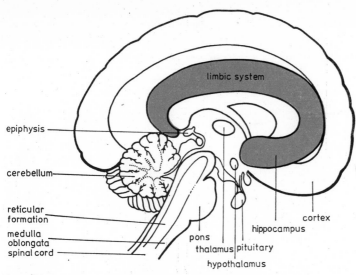

Fig. 43. The limbic system (in red) in the hidden medial zone of the cerebral hemispheres.

obvious contribution of unconscious emotional factors to human behavior.

Subsensory phenomena also belong to the realm of unconscious psychic processes. It has been shown by Gersuni **Subsensory phenomena** that conditioned reflexes can also be built upon stimuli which remain below the threshold of the receptive cortical area and therefore do not cause subjective sensations. An example of such a stimulus is a sound generator adjusted to a frequency which changes the electrical activity of the brain but is not heard by the subject.

Let us again refer to interoceptive visceral impulses **Interoception** which, as has been seen, reach the higher centers without eliciting subjective sensation. At the same time, interoceptive impulses profoundly influence animal and human behavior. "Vague sensations" arising from the viscera were described by Sechenov as early as 1866. For lack of a better

155

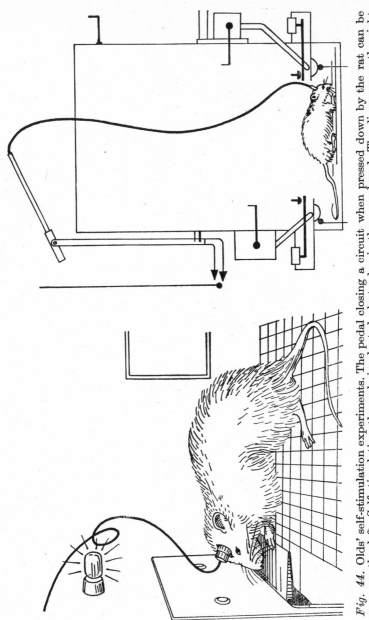

Fig. 44. Olds' self-stimulation experiments. The pedal closing a circuit when pressed down by the rat can be seen on the left. Self-stimulation through implanted electrodes is thus produced. The diagram on the right shows another experimental arrangement with pedals at the opposite ends of the chamber. One serves for getting food, the other for closing the electric circuit.

Fig. 45. Delgado's remote control experiment. Limbic or hypothalamic stimuli are delivered through the short-wave radio set built into the animal's collar. The response was either aggressive or friendly behavior.

definition, these sensations were collectively termed "general condition" or visceral sensation. Obviously, the totality of impulses arriving from visceral afferent pathways influence psychic activity through an unconscious mechanism.

In an experiment of ours volunteers swallowed a tube **Own studies** with an inflatable rubber balloon at the end. The tube was introduced into the upper part of the small intestine under fluoroscopic control. The balloon was inflated using a rubber bulb, and pressure in the balloon was controlled by a manometer. EEG electrodes were placed on the scalp of the prone, relaxed subject. When resting alpha activity appeared, stimulation of the intestine was started: by inflating the balloon, the intestinal wall was painlessly distended. This interoceptive stimulus led to the disappearance of alpha activity and to EEG desynchronization in all subjects, showing that intestinal stimulation caused reticular activation just like exteroceptive stimuli. The subjective experience of the experimental subjects was compared with the EEG changes. In 70% of the cases the subjects did not feel anything: the reticular arousal was not accompanied by subjective sensation. In 30% there was a vague sensation of tension; pain was felt only exceptionally.

In another series the subjects swallowed a tube with a double balloon. There was a distance of 15–20 cm between the two balloons, which were inflated independently. The pressure in the two balloons was also controlled separately. The EEG records in these experiments showed that the higher centers discriminated between the stimulation of the two intestinal segments (Fig. 46). No subjective feelings were reported by the subjects in these experiments either. The results have shown that visceral impulses influence the activity of central nervous structures without becoming conscious and that reticular activation and conscious activity are connected with different mechanisms.

Conscious activity, although requiring increased reticular function, is not the same as arousal: the diffuse waking reaction does not mean conscious sensation. This has also been shown by our experiments.

Making visceral impulses conscious As already mentioned, the impulses arriving from two visceral receptor zones are learned by the child to be controlled consciously. As a result of learning, tension in the urinary bladder and rectum become subjective sensations and their emptying is controlled accordingly. Based on this experience, we tried to make the intestinal impulses enter consciousness by way of conditioning. The experimental setup was the same as above. The subject swallowed the

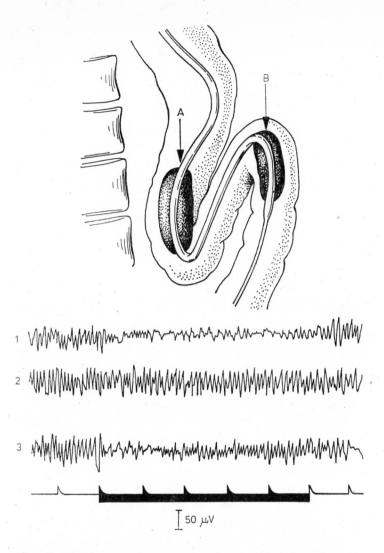

Fig. 46. Higher nervous centers are able to discriminate between impulses arising in intestinal segments 15–20 cm apart. Inflation of balloon A produces typical alpha blockade (1). Repeated stimulation leads to habituation (2). The electrical activity of the brain is again changed when, after habituation, balloon B is inflated (3). Calibration of time trace: 1 sec. The thick block below indicates stimulation.

159

tube with the balloon, the EEG electrodes were attached to his scalp, and the stimulus threshold of desynchronization of alpha activity (objective threshold) was determined. Then the pressure on the intestinal wall was further increased, by 5–10 mm Hg at a time, to find the pressure value at which the subject felt abdominal tension. This was regarded as the subjective threshold. Then pressure was reduced in steps of 10 mm Hg, but this time the pressure stimuli were associated with verbal stimuli like "stimulus applied now" or "now you will feel your stomach distending." After 20–30 such associations, the subjects reported subjective sensation of tension far below the earlier subjective threshold. In other words, by verbal reinforcement the subjects were taught to become conscious of intestinal stimuli that had been unconscious before the conditioning procedure. In these experiments we thus reproduced the process in the course of which the child learns to become aware of impulses arising in the bladder and rectum.

The question arises whether such conditioning as a result of which visceral impulses enter consciousness may occur naturally. The answer we can give today is that a whole series of visceral components of vital functions (hunger, thirst, urination, defecation) are, by way of conditioning, learned to be consciously perceived in early childhood. Conscious sensation of visceral stimuli other than those mentioned should be considered pathological or at least burdensome for the higher centers.

Another example of learning to consciously perceive visceral functions by way of conditioning, similar to our experiments, is when after a long period of illness cardiac patients become aware of even the smallest oxygen deficiency of the cardiac muscles. It might therefore be stated that visceral impulses should remain unconscious in healthy humans. Our opinion in this respect is similar to that mentioned in connection with Freudian psychoanalysis, namely, that bringing instinctive, unconscious processes into con-

160

sciousness may help to cure some diseases, but may, at the same time, lead to unwanted complexes or to neurosis. We know of cases in psychoanalytical practice when the attention of unsuspecting patients was called to nonexistent complexes connected, e.g., with their parents. Therapeutic forgetting is often more beneficial than bringing unconscious processes into consciousness.

The biology of the conscious state: an unknown field

Having read the foregoing section, the nonbiologist reader may be justified in asking a peculiar question: If such a great number of important visceral events and psychic processes occur outside consciousness, what is there left in the conscious sphere and what mental processes define the conscious state? We tried to answer this question at the beginning of this chapter, and only wish to add that the majority of sensory and motor functions connected with the *environment* (input or information uptake vs. output of instructions in the computer language, and *somatic* afferent vs. efferent functions in the physiological nomenclature) are conscious. Awareness is thus primarily extended to pieces of information from the outside world which are reflected by subjective sensations and the processing of which results in activity, mostly voluntary movement.

The contents of the conscious state:

Perception — conscious activity

Moreover, we are also aware of a whole series of psychic phenomena that are not directly connected with sensory and motor function. We experience some emotion (joy, pain, etc.) and are, at the same time, aware of it. (Naturally, there are also unconscious sensations, as has been described.) We may remember something and immediately know that we are remembering, etc. The conscious state thus implies that we are aware of our own mind. This superimposed phenomenon of awareness of being aware is the basis **Self-consciousness** of self-consciousness. In connection with our sensations, actions, and mental experiences we are aware of the existence and unity of our personality. The psychophysical methods described at the beginning of this book make use of this human capacity, called introspection.

The question arises how the human ability to be aware of psychic processes connected with the environment has developed. As mentioned earlier in this chapter, consciousness implies the synchronous appearance of events in the form of speech or thought ("internal speech").

In the early history of mankind there must have occurred **Secondary** a qualitative change in communication, surpassing the **signaling system** sign language of animal communities. This must have happened when the need arose for *articulate human speech* in connection with primitive social life and collective work (Fig. 47). The evolution of the speech function meant, at the same time, the appearance of consciousness. The language of primitive people is extremely direct: all natural phenomena are called by different names. For instance, there are different words for rainy weather, clear weather, and sunny weather, the abstraction of "weather" being unknown. Such languages, similar to animal sounds, are monosyllabic, and unconscious emotional elements dominate in them. From this unconscious, monosyllabic, concrete, emotional speech our conscious, articulate, abstract, and rational speech has developed in the course of more differentiated working activity and social development. We cannot deal here with the physiology of speech, but we might mention that by learning the first words (secondary signals) denoting basic environmental stimuli, the child takes the first steps toward abstraction. By saying "window" he does not only refer to a familiar object but to all the similar ones he can perceive with the help of the primary signaling system.

162

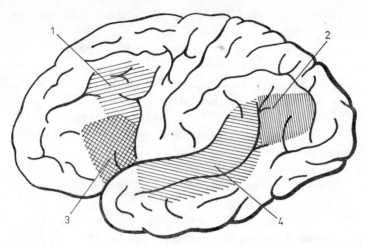

Fig. 47. Cortical localization of the speech function. Lesions of different cortical regions cause disturbances of (1) writing, (2) reading, (3) articulate speech, and (4) the understanding of speech.

The physiological basis of the generalization of secondary signals should be sought in the process of irradiation and generalization of excitation in cerebral neurons. All new words learned by the child trigger such a mechanism. When we express the general qualities of environmental objects, words become concepts by a process of *abstraction.* Concepts arise as a result of the selection of essential traits and relations from among the nonessential ones. In the brain this occurs as a concentration of excitation. Thus the biological basis of abstraction is the irradiation and concentration in cerebral neurons of newly formed signals that have been expressed in speech form.

According to most authors, the conscious thoughts of man which are not expressed in words may be regarded as "internal speech." Excitations belonging to the secondary signaling system do arise in this case, too, but will not give rise to motor responses, i. e., motor functions necessary for intonation (in the pharynx, tongue, facial muscles, etc.)

will not be activated. Consciousness is thus related to the secondary signaling system.

The reader wanting to learn about the energetics of the human mind may have been surprised that this part of our book offers only speculations rather than well-established biological facts as do other parts of the book. The reason for this is the lack of data that would enable us to formulate a physiological theory of consciousness. Even the available fragmentary data have not all been completely verified. Such data are, e.g., clinical observations leading to the postulation of a connection between consciousness and the frontal or parietal lobes of the cortex.

The last several years have brought considerable changes in the theories relating to consciousness. The available data, although still resembling unidentified pieces of a jigsaw puzzle, suggest that a drastic revision of current ideas on the mechanism of cerebral information processing is needed.

Since the late 1960's Roger Sperry has published a series of papers on some patients in whom the entire fiber system connecting the two cerebral hemispheres had to be surgically transected for therapeutic reasons. The corpus callosum between the two hemispheres contains about 200 fibers and has the function of coordinating the activity of symmetric cerebral centers. When this bundle of fibers is transected, the two hemispheres become independent information processing centers.

No striking differences between these patients with a "split" brain and normal individuals were found nor did their speech, verbal intelligence, memory, movements, and emotions, i.e., their whole personality, change as compared with their presurgery self. However, when the processing of visual information arriving from the left or right visual field, the perception of sound stimuli delivered to the right or left ear, or the tactile sensations arising as a result of touching an object with one of the hands were analyzed making use of specialized equipment, conspicuous

164

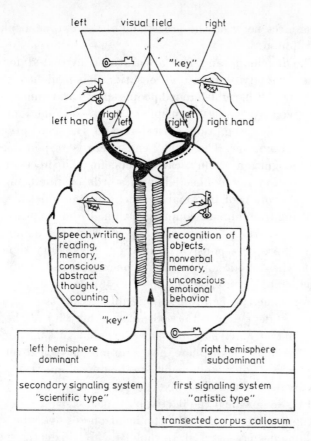

Fig. 48. Sperry's findings in patients with "split brain." After severing the connection between the hemispheres, conscious, abstract thinking and processing of verbal information can be traced to the dominant hemisphere, while the concrete reflection of the environment and the perception of information with emotional coloring is the business of the other, the subdominant hemisphere.

differences between the processing of the two hemispheres were found.

The ingenious and fine apparatus constructed for the separate study of unilateral sensations has made it possible to show that in right-handed people speech and numbers are perceived by the left hemisphere, to whose functions also belong the recognition of letters and the perception of abstract notions. The right hemisphere is responsible for the recognition of physical objects, for the processing of information not connected with words or numbers, and the perception of information with an emotional coloring resulting from human communication. In left-handed people the situation is reversed. It appears that the "dominant" hemisphere is responsive to abstract "secondary signals," while the "subdominant" hemisphere responds primarily to concrete "primary signals" (Fig. 48). If the connections between the two hemispheres are intact, this lateralization is not evident due to the coordinating activity of the rich fiber network. It may be, however, that in some people the "verbal" hemisphere has a dominant role over the "nonverbal" one, while in others the opposite is true. Even Pavlov distinguished between people of a "scientific" type and those he called the "artistic" type.

The dominance of one of the hemispheres over the other has long been recognized. In 1860 Broca localized the speech center of right-handed persons in the left hemisphere (see Fig. 47). As early as 1874, Jackson discovered the role of the contralateral hemisphere in the harmonizing of visual sensations. Modern surgical and experimental techniques have then made it possible to explore the respective roles of the severed hemispheres. The recently discovered laws of hemisphere specialization may lead to a breakthrough in consciousness research as well. It may turn out that a specific interaction between the masses of information processed by the two hemispheres separately is a prerequisite of consciousness.

Part III

The experience of the mind: learning and memory

In Parts I and II the route of information arriving from the environment or from the inside of the body has been traced to different levels of the brain, and the processing of these impulses has been discussed. Two mechanisms by which the information entering the input channels is transmitted to the cerebral neurons have been mentioned. One is the system of specific sensory pathways with a sensation as an "end-product", and the other is the nonspecific brain-stem reticular system controlling wakefulness, i.e., the energetics of information processing.

There is a third mechanism involved in information processing in addition to these two: environmental stimuli also trigger learning and storing processes in the brain. As a result, the range and direction of the function of cerebral neurons may change. In other words, the brain triggers and maintains extremely plastic and flexible functions to serve environmental adaptation. This third property of the information processing system, the ability to *accumulate past experience*, probably best equips the central nervous system for environmental adaptation.

This "triple route" of information forms an intricately interrelated system: there is no true sensation without awareness or without the emergence of memory traces,

The triple route of information

and also the function of memory is dependent on sensation and wakefulness.

The above-outlined third route will be dealt with in the next few chapters. The biology of learning and memory is currently in vogue. This may be attributed to two factors: (*i*) In most branches of science the cybernetic approach is gaining ground, and all control systems have memory units based on an analogy to biological memory functions. (*ii*) At various social and scientific levels we come up against the problem of learning, i.e., of mastering and storing the rapidly growing mass of information.

The physiology of learning and the mechanisms of recording and storing information, which are the most important brain functions for obtaining experience, will be discussed.

Chapter 10

Contiguity of cerebral processes: learning

The majority of sensory mechanisms — being innate — serve adaptation in the same way throughout the life of the individual. Whenever the cornea of the eye is exposed to an air current or touched by a foreign body, the blinking reflex is produced in the same way in response to an impulse arising in the pain receptors of the cornea. These forms of adaptation are genetically determined, and the reflexes are the same in all individuals of the species (e.g., man). These reflexes are called unconditioned.

However, the sensory pathway also participates in reflex activity of the acquired type, which develops in the individual during his life. The fixed system of innate, *unchanging* reflexes proved to be insufficient for survival in the course of phylogeny in the face of a changing environment. For instance, it is late for an animal to start defending itself when it has already been grabbed by its enemy. Therefore, certain behavioral functions that were more plastic than the unconditioned reflexes and which enabled the animal to adapt to the constant changes of the environment developed. Such reflexes come about whenever impulses arrive at the brain from different pathways more or less simultaneously. This means that the conditioned reflexes result from the contiguity of cerebral events. Various

Unconditioned and conditioned stimuli

normally irrelevant stimuli (noises, smells, shadows, etc.) may produce sensations which become associated with those arising in response to being attacked. Later on the associated "signals" will also trigger defensive behavior.

Conditioned reflex learning, which is often present in complex behavioral acts as a latent, hardly recognizable component, can be defined as belonging to one of the following two types (both reproducible under laboratory conditions): type I, learning by classical, or Pavlovian, conditioning, and type II, learning by operant conditioning.

Type I: Learning by classical conditioning

In describing the role of reflexes in behavior it is most expedient to follow Pavlov's reasoning. In young animals for a time after birth unconditioned reflex salivation can only be produced by putting the food into the animal's mouth (i.e., by chemically stimulating the taste buds). Later on *irrelevant* stimuli such as the color or odor of meat may *signal* the unconditioned (e.g., the relevant chemical) stimuli to the animal, or it may respond with salivation to various associated light or olfactory stimuli. This reaction is no longer innate (it never occurs in milk-fed animals), but has to be learned by the animal.

Conditioned stimulus: a signal The impulses triggered by an unconditioned stimulus (e.g., the chemical stimulus of meat) may reach the specific cerebral neurons at the same time as impulses elicited by another, irrelevant stimulus (e.g., the odor of the meat); several such coincidences will turn the neutral stimulus into a signal able to produce the automatic response (e.g., salivation) by itself.

172

Natural conditioned reflexes, such as the one described above, develop in the course of the animal's life. On the other hand, artificial conditioned responses may be established under laboratory conditions using special equiment. This process is called conditioning. In its simplest form food is given to the animal and a sound stimulus is presented at the same time. After a few trials, the sound (buzzer) alone will start the salivary process.

In these experiments *two sensory systems* of the animal are activated simultaneously: the subcortical and cortical auditory areas are the target of the sound stimulus and the medullary, thalamic, and cortical representations are the target of the chemical (taste) stimulus. Both events may in themselves figure as unconditioned stimuli, as each may elicit an automatic response. Food will elicit motor or glandular responses, while the sound gives rise to the orienting reflex (turning toward the source of sound). The requirement of contiguity

If the impulses triggered by the two unconditioned stimuli reach the central structures simultaneously on several occasions, a particular interconnection between the two centers develops. The *direction* of the interconnection points toward the biologically more important, i. e., stronger reflex. For the above-mentioned association, the interconnection may be plotted as follows:

Organ of Corti	→	auditory pathway	→	auditory center	→	motor center	→	muscles (orienting reflex)
Taste receptor	→	sensory pathway for taste	→	sensory center for taste	→	center of salivation	→	salivary gland (salivation)

The biologically less important orienting reflex is abolished (habituation), and the sound stimulus elicits the stronger response connected with food intake. The newly es-

173

tablished reflex makes use of the efferent branch of the automatic, innate reflex arc. The essence of the learned reflex mechanism is the interconnection between central structures participating in the two kinds of response. But—as will be shown—this connection is temporary.

The new reflex fulfills the requirement of contiguity: it is the result of two different series of impulses reaching the higher centers simultaneously. The biologically less important stimulus assumes the role of a signal and becomes a conditioned stimulus which is able to convey the information content of the stronger unconditioned stimulus; the latter may be omitted when the association has been firmly established.

Type II: Instrumental (operant) learning

Another well-known example may serve to illustrate this form of conditioned reflex learning. While establishing the reflex, there is no association of stimuli, or presentation of conditioned stimuli. The experimental setup is such that the animal is either rewarded (by food) or punished (by pain) depending on whether or not it presses a lever. In the first few trials the pressing of the lever is the result of the spontaneous rambling activity of the animal. On the first occasion when such a random pressing of the lever occurs, food is given to the animal. This *reinforcement* will then result in fresh activity: the animal will press the lever in the hope of getting food. The frequency of motor responses is controlled by the experimental animal: whenever it wants to get food, it presses the lever. The slope of the cumulative curve shown in Fig. 49 indicates the frequency of the learned responses.

174

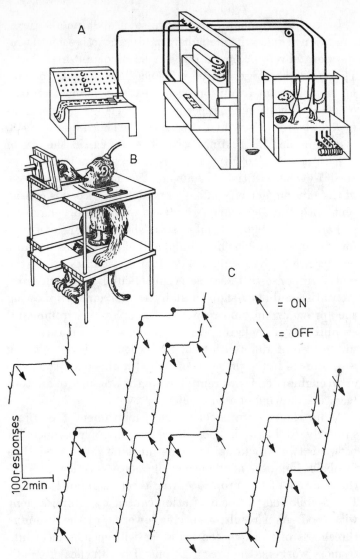

= ON

= OFF

100 responses

2min

Fig. 49. (A) Scheme of the experimental setup for classical conditioning. (B) Apparatus used for operant conditioning. The animal cannot move in the seat; electrodes have been implanted into its brain, and its viscera can be stimulated through indwelling tubes. Food is dispensed if the animal presses the lever. (C) Cumulative curve of learning showing the rate of lever pressing. There is no reinforcement with food during the period between the two arrows.

In the instrumental (operant, to use Skinner's term) conditioned reflex, there is invariably an active motor response, and reinforcement is the most important ingredient. The motor response can be influenced by the rate of reinforcing. Operant conditioning is clearly different from the classical conditioning experiments described above. This type of learning was first described by Thorndike in 1913, who explained his findings with what he called the *law of effect*. According to this law, the motor response is strengthened by the positive result, i.e., the food-getting effect, of the random activity of the animal. This theory is consistent with the Darwinian idea that only those behavioral patterns will become firmly established that are essential for the survival of the individual and of the species. It must be stressed that unlike Pavlovian conditioning, the motor response in this case is not elicited by an environmental stimulus or signal but by reinforcement following the previous motor response. Complex environmental stimuli play a background role, assuming importance only in the case of differentiation, e.g., when the lever pressing is reinforced in the presence of one stimulus (e.g., the noise of an engine) and is not reinforced in the presence of another (e.g., the blowing of a whistle).

As for the cerebral mechanism of instrumental learning, similarly to Pavlovian learning, a temporary connection between two functional systems must be postulated. The feedback impulses of the orienting motor activity activate the neurons of the proprioceptive cerebral representation. This is followed by the excitation caused by reinforcement with food. As a result, a specific lowering of the stimulus thresholds of the two central areas will ensue. According to most workers, the preconditions of both types of conditioned reflex learning are the same: the more or less simultaneous excitation of two distinct cerebral areas (Fig. 50).

The sequence of the two stimuli is not significant in either type. In classical conditioning the conditioned stimulus

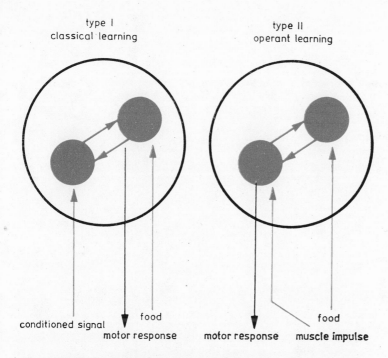

Fig. 50. Both classical and operant learning can be explained by the theory of contiguity.

may be presented after the unconditioned stimulus as long as the contiguity of the cerebral processes is ensured.

The development of operant conditioned reflexes is most probably connected with the fulfillment of some physiological need (e.g., hunger) in the course of reinforcement. According to Hull, for a behavioral pattern to become firmly established, there must be the drive to satisfy a basic need in the background. The motor response motivated by the drive fulfills the need and thereby reduces the strength of the drive. This question will be discussed later on.

Based on the work of Skinner, the process of learning by operant conditioning has been applied in different fields of human activity. Recent theories of programmed teaching **Programmed learning: gambling-machines** also contain the elements of these reflexes, since the positive feedback of the student is employed for reinforcement. Reinforcement programs have also been used in devising different gambling-machines: the gambler is occasionally rewarded (reinforced) with a prize to keep up his interest in the game, but the frequency of lever pressing (or coin inserting) must be high enough to assure a profit to the owners.

Faulty learning: superstitions Skinner also studied the biological background of superstitions and found that behavioral patterns resembling various superstitions in man can be found in animals. He found the reason to be some faulty cerebral connection, i. e., irrelevant learned behavior.

Superstitious pigeons Unjustified, random reinforcement (rewarding) may lead to "superstitious" behavior in animal experiments. The following experimental situation may serve to illustrate this random process. A pigeon is placed in a Skinner box having illuminated disks of different colors on one of its walls. The same wall also has an opening through which food is dispensed to the animal whenever it pecks at, e.g., the red disk. After a few trials the pigeon will peck at the red disk with increasing frequency, and an operant conditioned reflex will be established. The food dispensing can be set to occur after a certain number of peckings, say after 20 or 50, and the animal will learn to adapt itself to this frequency of reward. The pecking rate will be found to be fairly regular and the motor response will only be suspended for the period of food getting, and will be resumed thereafter. This pattern of behavior may be sustained for several days. If by some fault of the automatic food dispenser the animal gets an unexpected food reward following a random movement of its right leg, the pigeon will try to repeat this movement again and again because in the higher centers the motor pattern and its effect (food getting) have already become interconnected. This in short is an animal model of superstitious behavior.

178

We also have observed superstitious behavior in experimental monkeys. The animal had to press a lever 25 times to get a piece of candy from a metal tube fixed about 10 cm from its mouth. Once when the animal accidentally touched the tube with its mouth, a piece of candy dropped in front of it at a time when food should not have been dispensed had the automatic dispenser not been faulty because this was not the 25th lever pressing. This random reinforcement encouraged the animal to try to reach for the tube with its mouth, and we could observe this "superstitious" response for a long time afterwards.

The analogy with human superstitious behavior is self-evident. Such superstitious behavioral patterns have frequently been observed by teachers and psychologists in children, especially in puberty, a period of intensive learn- **Human analogies?** ing. The emotional state of anxiety is involved in humans (and probably also in animals) in the development of these phenomena. Superstitious associations are known to arise when there is fear or anxiety in the background, their aim being to get rid of fear. Superstitious beliefs based on erroneous causalities are handed down from one generation to the next and crop up under similar circumstances time and again. An innocent manifestation of such a make-believe causality is the carrying of good-luck charms or wearing of the same piece of clothing by students sitting for examinations.

The process of conditioning

The process of the development of operant conditioned responses will be clear from what has been described above. An accidental motor pattern is followed by rewarding, and this reinforcement will lead to repetition of the motor pattern with gradually increasing frequency. The process is different in classical conditioning.

Technique of conditioning

The practice adopted for establishing classical conditioned reflexes in Pavlovian experiments has been to deliver the two stimuli *simultaneously*. One of the stimuli is irrelevant from the point of view of the expected response. This stimulus will later on become the conditioned signal. The other stimulus given at the same time, which is called the unconditioned or reinforcing stimulus, elicits a well-defined response. After a few of these associations, the conditioned stimulus will by itself elicit the response, which by this time may be regarded as a learned, conditioned response. Traditionally the conditioned stimulus is presented simultaneously with the unconditioned one, or precedes it by a few seconds. However, it has recently been found that, in contrast to earlier theories, the conditioned connection will also come about if the stronger unconditioned stimulus precedes the weaker conditioned signal, i.e., a reverse association is also possible. At subsequent trials there may be a gradually increasing delay in the presentation of the unconditioned reinforcing stimulus, and the isolated effect of the conditioned stimulus can be registered.

To eliminate unnecessary orienting responses elicited by the interference of environmental stimuli, conditioned reflex experiments are performed in special sound- and light-proof chambers. Recently electrical shielding has also been added. The experimenter is seated at an automatic control table in a room adjacent to the experimental chamber, and from there controls the parameters of the stimuli and registers the responses of the experimental subject. In recent years a wide range of different experimental setups have been used in different neurophysiological and psychological laboratories to study conditioning. As has been indicated at the beginning of our book, besides the modern electrophysiological methods of stimulation and action

180

potential recording, the learning tests are the most useful means of studying higher nervous activity.

In the course of classical conditioning the irrelevant weak stimulus initially elicits the orienting reflex first described by Pavlov: the animal turns in the direction of the stimulus, is aroused, etc. This innate investigative reaction appears in response to every unexpected stimulus and is known to be connected with the function of the brainstem reticular system. When a conditioned reflex is established, the orienting response to the conditioned stimulus disappears: it is habituated. Habituation is a precondition of conditioned reflex activity. The conditioned reflex becomes "neutral" in the course of habituation, and as a result of association of the stimulus with a stronger unconditioned stimulus a temporary connection between the afferent (sensory) branch of the orienting reflex arc and the efferent (motor) branch of the strong unconditioned reflex arc develops. The orienting reflex thus belongs to the early phase of conditioning; its appearance and extinction precede the formation of the temporary interconnection of different cerebral structures.

There is ample experimental evidence showing that whenever two excitations in two distinct groups of cerebral neurons coincide, there is a ringlike *propagation* of excitation from one area to the other. In this manner the stimulus thresholds of both neuronal groups are lowered, i.e., facilitation occurs. The first phase of temporary connection is no doubt characterized by reflex facilitation occurring between the two central groups of neurons. As a result, the conditioned reflex will, after a few associations, elicit the conditioned response, but the reflex is still weak and may disappear after a few elicitations, since it is merely based on a lowering of the stimulus threshold of the two centers as a result of the propagation of excitation.

This early, labile form of conditioned response was called summation reflex by Pavlov. Others have called it *sensiti-*

181

zation, and it has been maintained that lower species of the animal kingdom, mainly invertebrates, are capable of only this type of summation or sensitization response.

Automatisms   Further associations after the development of the summation response establish the reflex quite firmly, so that elicitation after longer intervals (a day or longer) as well as differentiation are also possible. At this stage the responses may be regarded as a true conditioned reflex. Evidence has been presented in recent years indicating that there are particularly strong conditioned connections which will not be extinguished throughout the subject's lifetime, even without reinforcement. These are learned automatisms serving the purpose of defense in various animals. For example, it has been shown by Knoll that if a rat is dropped onto a metal plate into which electric current has been conducted, the animal will jump off the plate. After a few of such painful stimuli the rat will jump off the metal plate as long as it lives even if there are no subsequent reinforcements, i. e., if the animal is not exposed to any further electric shock. Conditioned reflexes exhibit a wide range of firmness—from the weak summation reflex to the learned automatisms which are preserved for life. The grades of firmness are difficult to delimit, and no objective criteria for such a differentiation are likely to be found.

Structural organization of conditioned reflexes

Spinal learning   Learning processes resulting from the simultaneous excitation of two groups of neurons have been demonstrated at all levels of the central nervous system. Simple learned responses have been described in animals deprived of

182

their cerebrum, midbrain, and medulla but with the spinal cord intact. The spinal processes proved to be fairly labile summation reflexes but nevertheless were learned responses.

We have also performed experiments with rats and cats Midbrain cats whose brainstem had been transected above the midbrain. We succeeded in showing that conditioned reflexes can be established in midbrain cats surviving decerebration by a few weeks (Fig. 51). Although these experiments failed to throw light on the finer mechanisms of this kind of connection, the brainstem reticular system may be postulated to take part in the development of primitive conditioned reflexes. The learned respiratory response established in these experiments proved to be a summation reflex:

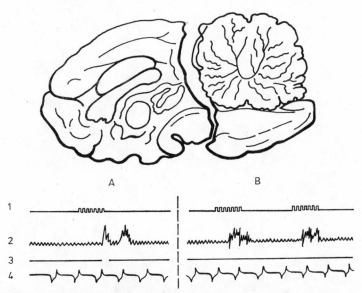

Fig. 51. Respiratory conditioned response in cats deprived of their cerebrum, i.e., having only midbrain, medulla, and spinal cord. The plane of transection is shown at the top. (A) Respiratory reflex in controls. (B) The same learned response persists after transection of the brainstem: 1, conditioned sound stimulus; 2, conditioned respiratory response; 3, unconditioned electric shock; 4, time calibration, 1 sec.

183

though numerous associations were needed for its establishment, it did not persist for longer than 24 hours without reinforcement. It has thus been proved that the brainstem is suitable for the establishment of associative processes, just as the spinal cord has been found to be.

It has been known ever since the work of Pavlov that conditioned reflexes can be established in decorticated dogs, but these responses are extremely labile, of variable intensity, and resemble summation reflexes. It is possible to build simple learned responses on light and auditory stimuli **Contiguity at all** in decorticated animals, but instrumental reactions re- **levels** quiring more complex activity cannot be accomplished without the cerebral cortex.

Comparative physiological studies have yielded data on the development of learned connections in lower animal species having no cortex. Temporary connections have been observed in all invertebrates. Moreover insects may exhibit true conditioned reflex behavior. Lasting conditioned reflexes may be found in all vertebrates, ranging from fishes to man. These reflexes, however, disappear if the animal is deprived of the highest nervous structure characterizing the given species. For example, learned processes disappear in bees after the supra-esophageal ganglion, the bee's most important nervous center, is destroyed.

Based on this evidence it is generally held today that the highest cerebral structure of the species is involved in the development of conditioned responses. In mammals the cerebral cortex plays an important although not exclusive role in more complex conditioned learning processes. Less intricate reflexes in mammals and also in man may be established in lower nervous structures, from the spinal cord to the thalamus. In theory, *all* levels of the central nervous system may become sites of learning processes by virtue of the contiguity in time of excitation.

Terminological It may be asked whether such spinal, midbrain or tha-
discrepancy lamic processes can be regarded as conditioned reflexes in

184

the classical Pavlovian sense, but this is more or less a problem of semantics. The mechanisms of the summation reflex and the true conditioned reflex are the same. The summation reflex is the *initial* stage of learning, becoming gradually firmer with repeated reinforcement. To draw a line between the different stages would be just as difficult as the differentiation of learned automatisms from conditioned reflexes requiring reinforcement (see above). The system formed by the complex behavioral patterns in the central nervous system is not a horizontal one confined to different levels (cortex, thalamus, midbrain, etc.), but shows vertical organization. The activities of different cortical and sub-cortical groups of neurons may thus be identified as ingredients of complex processes of learning.

The negative reflection of learning: inhibition

Conditioned connections are not only constantly established in the brain, but, being temporary, are also abolished all the time. Inhibition arising at the same time as excitation during learning is responsible for the transitory character of conditioned reflexes. Pavlov himself found many inhibitory processes in higher nervous centers wich occur simultaneously with excitation. When excitation wanes, inhibition gains ground, and the other way around. The plasticity of complex behavioral patterns is maintained by the dynamism of the two forms of activity. This phenomenon has been called the functional mosaic of the cerebral hemispheres by Pavlov.

On the neuronal level inhibition is due to hyperpolarization of the cell membrane (see p. 201). In the hyperpolarized

Inhibition: hyperpolarization

185

state the negativity of the inside of the cell increases with respect to the surrounding fluid even further, and thus the polarity and firing threshold of the membrane increases. The hyperpolarizing effect is transmitted to the central nervous system through inhibitory *synapses* (see p. 201). These inhibitory interneural connections may prevent the propagation of excitation. Experiments with microelectrodes have shown that a single nerve cell may receive and transmit both excitatory and inhibitory impulses through different input and output channels. Besides, several cell types are known in the central nervous system the main function of which is the transmission of inhibitory hyperpolarizing impulses. Thus all cerebral neurons may have an inhibitory function, but in addition there are specialized cells playing an exclusively inhibitory role.

External inhibition The simplest form of inhibition is due to a sudden new stimulus causing excitation at the time of the conditioned reflex. In this case the conditioned stimulus does not elicit the learned response. This is due to the unexpected stimulus triggering an orienting reflex which probably changes the direction of excitation and terminates the threshold-lowering connection between the two central areas. This is what we call external inhibition, a well-known everyday experience. For instance, if the attention of the reader is distracted by someone entering the room, the conditioned connection in the visual cortex established while reading this text is temporarily extinguished. External inhibition is independent of learning, being an inherited, innate form of activity.

Protective inhibition Superliminal or protective inhibition is another innate behavioral pattern. If the intensity of the conditioned stimulus surpasses a certain limit—the tolerance of the analyzer neuron—the excitatory state is suddenly switched over to protective inhibition. The aim of this inhibitory activity is no doubt the protection of the receptors and cerebral centers from strain. Its mechanism is not known,

186

although several of its concomitants have been analyzed by Vedensky and his followers.

Most inhibitory phenomena connected with learning are "Negative" learning acquired and not innate. Such forms of inhibition might be called "negative" learning because they are acquired just like their positive counterparts, the conditioned responses. Whenever there is excitation in only one higher center instead of two for a prolonged period, an inhibitory process will invariably be initiated. In other words, this kind of inhibition occurs if reinforcement of the conditioned stimulus by an unconditioned stimulus is omitted. All conditioned stimuli may cause inhibition if applied alone over a prolonged period. Pavlov called this phenomenon internal inhibition. It is a learned pattern of behavior similar to the conditioned reflexes it interferes with.

Extinction is the most important manifestation of ac- Extinction quired inhibition, occurring whenever reinforcement of the conditioned stimulus is omitted on several occasions. The conditioned response becomes gradually weaker, and in due course the signaling stimulus elicits no reaction at all. At this point the conditioned reflex may be regarded as extinguished. The speed of extinction is inversely related with the intensity of the unconditioned and conditioned stimuli applied: stronger stimuli produce more lasting connections and the other way around. Extinction might probably be attributed to termination of the contiguity of the two excitations in the respective higher centers. By some unknown mechanism, the conditioned stimulus which is able to elicit a response without reinforcement also triggers impulses which eventually lead to inhibition. Inhibition causing extinction is an important biological function as it helps to abolish conditioned responses not involved in defensive behavior. If a signal is no longer relevant to a biologically important innate reaction (e.g., feeding), its persistence would be harmful from the point of view of adaptation. Extinction thus helps to eliminate unnecessary cerebral functional connections.

Disinhibition   Acquired inhibition—e.g., extinction—is not simply the dissipation of a pattern of excitation, but an active process with a negative sign. To prove this statement, Pavlov devised his ingenious experiments of disinhibition, or inhibition of the inhibition. Sudden new stimuli are also able to inhibit the process of extinction through the mechanism of **external** inhibition. For instance, a dog is conditioned to a light stimulus; then the response is extinguished by withholding the reinforcing unconditioned stimulus of food. At this stage a new unexpected stimulus (e.g., the sound of a buzzer) coinciding with the light stimulus will cause the conditioned response to reappear due to a switch from inhibition to excitation. The experiment clearly proves that the animal does not "forget" the response, it is merely inhibited. Thus the phenomenon of disinhibition is suitable for proving the active character of inhibition even if the structural background of these phenomena is still inaccessible to the neurophysiologist.

Differentiation   Extinction plays a part in other forms of acquired inhibition as well. For instance, if a conditioned reflex of salivation is established to the sound of a bell and a buzzer is also set off at the time of the response, this latter stimulus, owing to the propagation of excitation, will also trigger the conditioned reflex on the first few trials. If the bell is invariably reinforced with food but the buzzer is not, salivary response to the bell will persist, but that to the buzzer will gradually be extinguished. The buzzer thus has become a negative stimulus causing extinction. This type of inhibition may be explained by the higher centers being able to distinguish between reinforced and unreinforced stimuli which otherwise send impulses to the same central areas. This so-called differential inhibition was instrumental in the discovery of important phenomena in neurophysiology.

As has been described in dealing with the investigative methods used in the study of the sense organs, tests applying the phenomenon of differential inhibition are of special

188

importance. Findings such as the inability of dogs to distinguish different colors, dogs being sensitive only to variations in light intensity, are due to this test method. It has also been found that dogs can discriminate clockwise from counterclockwise movement, or a crotchet from a quaver. Differential inhibition is an important cerebral function since it helps in discriminating various environmental stimuli. Its neuronal mechanism has been discussed in the chapter dealing with sensory function. Extinction and differentiation are only the most important facets of inhibition; other forms are also encountered in learning processes, but these will not be discussed here.

Acquired inhibition invariably develops in response to sustained monotonous stimuli. As has been mentioned earlier, such monotonous stimuli also play a role in the development of sleep. If a single stimulus causes excitation of a cerebral sensory center over a prolonged period, internal inhibition develops; if stimulation is maintained over this stage, the local inhibitory processes will spread to other parts of the cerebral hemispheres, resulting in sleep. According to Pavlov, there is only a quantitative difference between internal inhibition and sleep, and the former may be regarded as partial sleep. Monotonous stimuli invariably produce a hypnotic state and then sleep, owing to the spreading of inhibition. Everyday experience also corroborates this theory. For example, a monotonous lecture, reading a dull book, or staying in a dim, quiet room (an environment poor in stimuli) inevitably causes drowsiness or, eventually, sleep.

Propagation of inhibition—sleep

Let us briefly revert to the phenomenon of differential inhibition. It has been said that the conditioned reflex can also be elicited by a stimulus that excites the same cortical area and differs from the true conditioned stimulus only slightly (e.g., bell and buzzer). This is due to irradiation, i.e., the spreading of excitation. If the original conditioned stimulus is reinforced, i.e., the original reflex

Irradiation—concentration

strengthened, but the differentiating stimulus is applied without reinforcement, differential inhibition develops. The cerebral concomitant of this process is the concentration of excitation to the area originally aroused by the first conditioned stimulus (the sound of the bell in our example). The process of concentration forms the basis of the differentiating ability of higher nervous centers. It is a general law that in the *early* phases of learning, excitation caused by the eliciting stimulus spreads to the neighboring cerebral areas. The reflex then is firmly established if excitation becomes concentrated in the group of neurons which is the central representation of the conditioned stimulus.

Negative induction   Thus a firmly established positive conditioned-response excitation elicits inhibition in the surrounding cerebral areas similarly to the excitatory and inhibitory areas found in the visual cortex. This specific cerebral contrast phenomenon is known in psychology as negative induction. The concentrated excitation is probably delimited from the inhibition prevailing in neighboring areas by means of negative induction. Moreover it is possible that external inhibition also rests on a similar mechanism: the new excitatory focus is surrounded by a zone of negative induction which includes both centers participating in the learning process, or at least one of them. Extremely strong inhibition may also give rise to processes of the opposite sign in surrounding areas, and this might be termed *positive induction*. There is an increasing tendency among neurophysiologists to hold intensive, stable excitatory or inhibitory states of cerebral neurons to be capable of triggering processes of the opposite sign in other neurons. These phenomena of induction or contrast may belong to the basic regularities of cerebral organization.

Learning in the living organism

Adaptation to the environment does not come about by way of simple conditioned reflexes, but is the result of a great number of different learned and innate responses forming a complex system with intricate connections among the ingredients. The complexity of natural conditioned reflexes is due to exposure to groups of stimuli rather than to individual stimuli. Conditioned connections of feeding or defense in animals are mostly *environmental reflexes*, as they are elicited by complex signals coming from the environment. If the sequence of the stimuli is constant on several occasions, the unconditioned or conditioned responses will also follow a *fixed sequence*. This may be such a firm fixation that the reflex may be elicited not by its conditioned stimulus, but by the response given to the preceding stimulus. Thus the *dynamic stereotypes*, the physiological basis of human habits, develop. Under normal conditions the more or less recently acquired stereotyped forms of adaptation occur together with innate automatic responses. The pioneers of behavioral research succeeded in analyzing this complex of patterns and to reproduce the individual ingredients under laboratory conditions as different models of learning. Such "pure forms" of learned responses rarely occur under natural conditions.

Complex behavioral patterns

The learning processes of living organisms are rendered extremely complex not so much by the intricately interconnected system of reflexes as by the fact that motivated conditioned responses, i.e., those having an emotional background, are more rapidly established and persist longer than those without a biological drive. According to some research workers, the only purpose of learning is the satisfaction of basic physiological needs, in other words, to reduce drive. This may be true for the second type, i.e., instrumental learning, but operant conditioning differs

Motivation

191

from the classical Pavlovian type just in that no drive reduction is necessary for the latter. The temporary connection between any two cerebral foci of excitation elicited by biologically less important stimuli results in learning even if neither is in connection with basic physiological needs. For instance, the experimental subject will learn to associate also indifferent groups of words and to respond to the "password" of the experimenter. Motivation also plays a role in classical conditioning in that, if conditioning is reinforced with reward or punishment, the reflex will be firmer and more lasting than in the case of the combination of biologically indifferent stimuli. The above-mentioned experimental subject will learn to associate the given words sooner if he is rewarded for successful learning and punished when he fails to learn the association. In view of these facts it is no wonder that the use of motivation has become so popular in various modern theories of teaching.

Chapter 11

The other aspect of cerebral plasticity: the fixing and storing of information

Learning and memory. These two words are regarded as almost synonymous by most people, and not without reason, as will be shown later on. Psychologically and biologically, however, there are considerable differences between the two. The differences will be scrutinized here from the biological aspect. After having described the phenomena of learning in the preceding chapter, we now wish to discuss some current problems of the fixing of memory traces.

It has been stressed that from the biological point of view learning is the coincidence of two conscious or unconscious processes in the brain. Memory is a less complicated process in one sense, but also more complicated in other aspects. It is simpler in the sense that for the early stage, i.e., fixing, it is sufficient for the neurons to receive a single train of impulses. These impulses effect a functional or structural change of some sort in the central neurons, producing what is called a *memory trace* or engram for lack of a better term. The mechanism of fixing of memory traces is a much studied problem because this is the phase most readily accessible with current experimental techniques. The entire psychic process of memory is much more complicated than learning, because it includes the mechanism of *recall*,

Learning and memory

of which we only know that it is based on associations similar to those in learning.

In one aspect memory is governed by the same rules as learning, and this is the importance of repetition. Just as learning rests on the repeated coincidence of combined stimuli, for a memory trace to come about, repetition of the same information is needed.

Theory of memory traces Several theories of memory have been advanced, but none of these lived as long as the currently favored one of memory traces. We have not yet discovered a more plastic or illustrative metaphor to describe the essence of memory than that of the waxen tablet used by Plato. All the expressions used to describe phenomena connected with memory recall his description (trace, imprinting, plasticity, etc.). In the age of magnetic signal-storing units this metaphor seems to have gained fresh impetus, and the scientist dealing with the biology of memory cannot help but make use of its elements when putting forward new hypotheses.

"Imprinting" The term imprinting is also used to denote a mechanism in animal behavior. The Austrian zoologist Lorenz hatched two groups of goose eggs, one group under the mother goose and the other one in an incubator. The goslings hatched by the goose followed their mother everywhere, whereas those hatched in the incubator first saw Lorenz when they were taken from the incubator and followed *him*. When he mixed the two groups of goslings under a big box, the two groups immediately sorted themselves out after the box was lifted off, as the animals recognized their "parents." This phenomenon occurring in animals at a very young age was called imprinting by Lorenz (Fig. 52). The freshly hatched animals imprint in their brain the first object that moves and gives a sound and follow it from that moment on. This phenomenon has not only been observed in birds, but also in insects, fishes, and even in some mammals. It can only be observed on the first day after birth. The reason for this is not known, but it has been postulated that

194

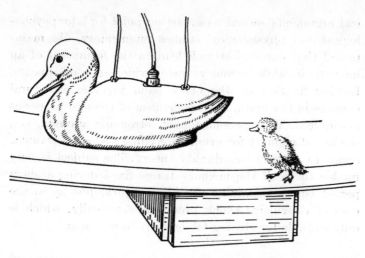

Fig. 52. In the process of "imprinting" the gosling follows every movement of the artificial mother goose, the first moving object it saw after hatching.

conditioned connections and emotional reactions (e.g., fear) developing later suppress this early imprinting mechanism, which is of special importance for the rest of the life of the animal. According to Hebb, the significance of imprinting lies in the fact that these early sensations may define the later behavior of the animal (or man). Interestingly, the result of imprinting depends not so much on the duration or the process as on the *effort* made by the animal when following the imprinted object. If the experimental court is strewn with obstacles the imprinting is more successful than if the gosling follows its natural or artificial mother on a surface that has been rolled smooth. The mechanism of this kind of imprinting must be similar to the fixing of memory traces by animals to be discussed later.

The Canadian Hebb has had an important part in shaping the current theory of memory traces. Based on the work of others before him, in 1949 he published a hypothesis on the duality of the imprinting of memory traces. His theoret- **"Dual process" theory** ical arguments served as a starting point for later psychological and physiological studies on memory. He maintained that external stimuli lead to the formation of an immediate labile memory trace, which soon disappears. Lasting fixation on the other hand involves structural changes in the brain. The mechanism of the two processes is different. The phenomenon of retrograde amnesia, i.e., the loss of memory for events preceding a cerebral trauma, seems to support this duality theory. The subject is only unable to recall the memory traces fixed during a short period before sustaining the brain injury, just as in the case of convulsive shock produced electrically, which is only suitable for erasing labile short-term traces.

Short-term (labile) memory

Closed neuron circuits   The hypothesis of the physiological mechanism of short-term memory has been based on morphological findings, which is a peculiar fact. It was reported by Forbes in 1920 that in addition to the open neuronal chains of the central nervous system, there exist intricate closed networks at all levels. His observations were used by Lorente de Nó, who precisely described the closed neuronal networks at different parts of the cerebral hemispheres. Based on this morphological description it was easy for physiologists to postulate a practically interminable *reverberation* of impulses needing no reinforcement by fresh sensory stimuli. These self-stimulating, so-called reverberating, circuits may form the basis of short-term memory (Fig. 53).

Self-stimulating circuit   Based on the morphological data, in 1938 Rashevsky devised a model of memory that consists of reverberating

196

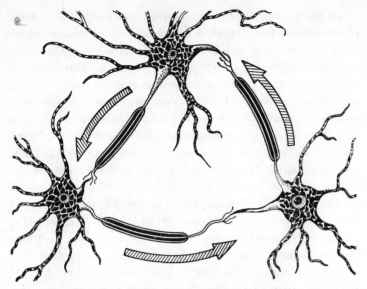

Fig. 53. Scheme of a reverberating neuronal circuit.

circuits in which trains of impulses circulate *without rein-forcement* for a long time. Fresh afferent impulses only intensify the wave of reverberating impulses. He also suggested that these circuits play a role in conditioning in addition to short-term memory. The impulse elicited by the new, conditioned stimulus is summed with the reverberating wave of depolarization, thus eliciting a conditioned response. Rashevsky also furnished mathematical evidence for his theory, which is still the starting point for modern theories of reverberation information storage. He applied his mathematical model to different psychological memory processes, but could not explain, in terms of this theory, the long-term memory strengthening with time, especially in old age.

The existence of self-stimulating circuits in the gray matter of the brain was proved only in the 1960's by Verzeano and Negishi, who introduced microelectrodes into several neurons of a small area of a few square millimeters. They observed a wave of impulses triggered by stimulation, which showed a delay in reaching the successive cells. The delay corresponded to the time needed for synaptic transmission.

Electric memory model

In our own experiments, likewise started in the 1960's, *conditioned evoked potentials* were registered in the cat's cortex, thalamus, and midbrain reticular formation in response to electric stimulation of afferent nerves. These learned evoked potentials were regarded as an electrical memory model. Without reinforcement the responses developed in one session soon disappeared. Thus they might be regarded as short-term, labile memory traces based on a reverberating wave of action potentials in a self-stimulating circuit of the pertinent group of cerebral neurons. To prove our hypothesis, electroconvulsive shock was applied.

Effect of electric shock

The electroshock treatment introduced by Cerletti and Bini has given rise to much debate in the literature. If a pulse of electricity of 120 V and 100–500 mA lasting 0.5–1 sec is introduced into the brain, an epileptoid convulsion is evoked. Such a shock treatment results in a complete loss of consciousness, lasting for about 3 minutes. For 30 minutes after the treatment, there is a gradually improving clouding of memory. The seizure lasts about one minute (tonic phase of a few seconds, followed by a clonic phase of 30 seconds). According to most authors, the high-frequency current pulse causes edema in the brain, leading to temporary loss of the synaptic connection between the neurons. In patients undergoing electroshock treatment there will be complete amnesia for the events of a very short period before the treatment, the memory of which will never return, indicating that the shock only interferes with short-term memory. McGaugh maintains that the electric shock severs the functional reverberating circuits. This might explain our experiments, in which electroshock treatment completely obliterated learned potentials produced in cats with relatively few paired stimuli (about 200) within one day. The results of our electrical experiments were thus interpreted as producing memory traces by establishing reverberating neuronal circuits. Sensory stimuli associated with a delay of 200–400 msec started a circular

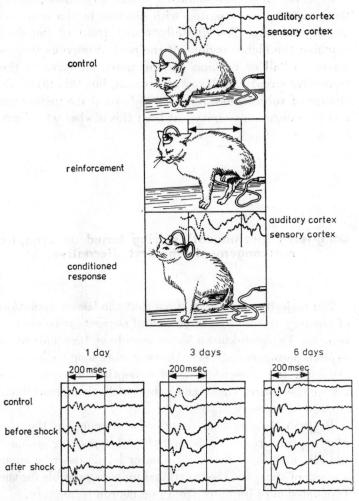

Fig. 54. Top, establishment of a delayed evoked potential in the cat. Bottom, the learned response can still be extinguished with electroshock after 1 day, but is permanently fixed after 3 and 6 days.

199

activity of corresponding periodicity. The reverberating train of impulses is digital, but the overall result is analog: the learned evoked potential produced by the summed post-synaptic potentials (Fig. 54).

In terms of the reverberating circuit hypothesis, short-term memory is connected with changes in the neuronal *membranes* only. The digitally coded train of impulses reaching the higher regions of the central nervous system starts an "all or nothing" action potential wave in the respective circular pathway of neurons, but this rhythmic change of voltage does not extend beyond the membrane and its immediate vicinity—at least this is what we believe today.

Long-term (permanent) storing based on synaptic rearrangement—the first alternative

The majority of authors agree that the lasting retention of memory traces requires *structural changes* in the central neurons. Two well-known hypotheses have been offered to explain permanent storage. One connects long-term memory with the strengthening of synaptic connections between the neurons and the other with the intracellular storage of memory traces.

In 1955 Szentágothai described differences in the size of synaptic surfaces in the spinal cord depending on their use. To make this discovery clearer let us describe some aspects of synapses, the functional units responsible for the transmission of impulses from one neuron to another.

The structure of synapses   The axons of one neuron contact the body or dendrite of the next neuron by means of the end bulbs. Both the

200

end bulb containing vesicles and the protoplasm of the next cell are bounded by membranes of approximately 50 Å thickness. Electron-microscopic examination has shown a gap of about 200 Å between the pre- and post-synaptic membranes. A special transmitter substance is stored in the presynaptic terminals. Each arriving impulse triggers the release of *transmitter substance* across the synaptic gap. It has been shown by electron microscopy that the substance is stored in the vesicles, some of which are open toward the synaptic gap.

Recording through electrodes introduced into the receiving postsynaptic neuron close to the membrane will show a resting state if there are no impulses arriving through the synapse. If the presynaptic fiber is stimulated, a potential difference between the two sides of the membrane will be recorded, which is called postsynaptic potential (PSP). The PSP is a *local* response and differs from the action potential by failing to show the all-or-nothing character of the latter and by being limited to the postsynaptic membrane. It is an analog sign able to generate a fresh train of action potentials in the membrane adjacent to it (Fig. 55).

PSP: analog sign

In some cells the transmitter substances only give rise to *hypopolarizing* PSPs, thereby reducing the resting potential. In others, other transmitters cause *hyperpolarizing* PSPs with an increased resting potential. Hyperpolarizing PSPs are excitatory, while the hyperpolarizing ones are inhibitory. As has been said, the PSP is a local phenomenon, is not transmitted, and only serves to trigger a train of action potentials in the next cell, just as the PSP itself is generated by an incoming signal, the action potential of the presynaptic cell. Thus at this point the transmission of nervous impulses occurs by a conversion of digital to analog signals, followed by a reconversion to digital ones.

Several kinds of transmitter substances have been postulated to be formed and stored in the vesicles of the syn-

Transmitters

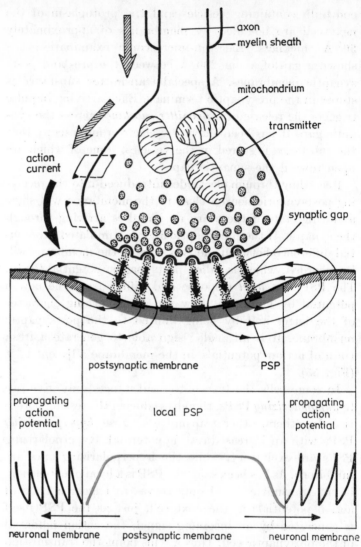

Fig. 55. Synaptic transfer of impulses. Postsynaptic changes brought about by mediator substances are shown in red (local PSP).

aptic end bulbs of the central nervous system. These may serve for the transmission of impulses or inhibition of transmission, respectively. Acetylcholine is the transmitter of excitatory impulses; by the injection of acetylcholine artificial hypopolarization can be produced. Gamma-aminobutyric acid (GABA) is regarded as an inhibitory transmitter.

The action potential of the presynaptic neuron is thus transmitted only to the end bulb of its axon, where it causes the release of the transmitter. The latter crosses the synaptic gap and lands on the membrane of the postsynaptic neuron, changing its ion permeability. Depending on the amount of transmitter, a stronger or weaker PSP is generated. If the PSP is hypopolarizing and sufficiently intensive, it will generate a periodic action potential transmitted in the outgoing axon of the second cell (Fig. 56). In terms of this theory, each neuron must have two kinds of membrane: the one opposite the end bulb and the membrane covering the rest of the cell. The same kind of duality has been encountered in the membranes of the receptors. The membrane of fibers within the receptor was shown to be capable of generating a local analog sign, while in the fiber outside the receptor a transmitted, all-or-nothing train of signals is found. Thus the PSP is a generator potential similar to the receptor potential at the input terminal of sensory impulses.

Two kinds of membrane

The time elapsed between the arrival of the presynaptic impulse at the end bulb and the generation of PSP, called synaptic delay, has been measured with the use of microelectrodes. It has been found to range from 0.3 msec to 3 msec in different animals. This delay has the following components: the period required for the release of the transmitter and those needed for the diffusion of this substance onto the postsynaptic membrane and for the generation of a PSP.

Synaptic delay

Let us now see the possible role of synapses in the storage of memory traces. The *absolute number* of synapses belong-

Synaptic growth

203

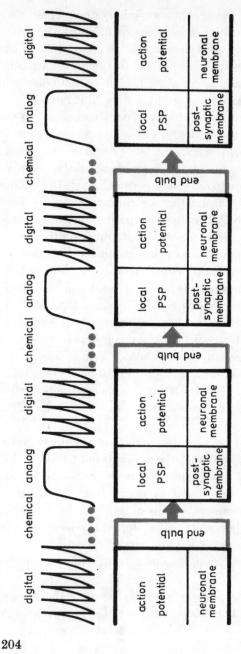

Fig. 56. Chemical transmission allowing analog-to-digital conversion in the course of propagation of nervous impulses.

ing to a single neuron as well as the *size* of the end bulbs are believed to depend on the use of the pathway they belong to. More strenuous use tends to increase these parameters, whereas they diminish when the pathway is out of action. This shows a good adaptive capacity of the impulse-transmitting apparatus. The changes in the size and weight of the synapses have been demonstrated by histological methods.

It has been shown by Eccles that the adaptive capacity More lasting PSPs of synapses in the higher nervous structures (brain) is superior to that of lower synapses, e.g., in the spinal cord or brainstem. The amplitude and duration of PSPs in the brain are about ten times those in the spinal cord, where PSPs are as a rule weak and of short duration (Fig. 57). Eccles therefore postulated that the intensive use of cerebral synapses results not only in an increase in the size of the interfaces, but also in that of the amount of transmitters, which then generate a longer lasting PSP.

The adaptive capacity of the synapse is shown by the Posttetanic potentiation experiments in which posttetanic potentiation (PTP) has been produced. As a result of electrical stimulation for several minutes using high-frequency current (tetanization), facilitation of the PSP, i.e., lowering of the threshold of

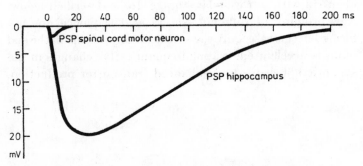

Fig. 57. Eccles' chart showing that PSPs in the brain are more permanent than in the spinal cord.

205

the postsynaptic membrane, occurs. An action potential will be generated in the postsynaptic cell in response to even subthreshold stimuli for several minutes after tetanization of the presynaptic cell. The neuron seems to "remember" the high-frequency stimuli that ceased coming in several minutes earlier. Such a mechanism is possibly involved in the synaptic process of the establishment of memory traces.

Summary: threefold change in the synapses There are thus three different properties of synapses known which might serve as the physiological basis of lasting retention of memory traces: the increase in size of the synaptic surfaces, the prolonged duration of PSPs, and the PTP-like lowering of threshold. All three may be involved in the property characteristic of cerebral neuronal pathways that they become more sensitive with increased use, when, one might say, they are "run in".

Accelerated protein synthesis No increase in the volume of end bulbs and in transmitter production by the vesicles can, however, be imagined without an acceleration of the complex intracellular molecular processes. Most important among these is no doubt the RNA-controlled protein synthesis. Data have been published in recent years indicating that the formation of polypeptide chains may play a role in the growth of synapses in response to their increased use. It must be stressed that this acceleration of protein synthesis is not identical with intracellular storage, to be described below. New proteins of different amino acid sequence are not formed in this case, only the synthesis of proteins in the end bulbs is accelerated, leading to quantitative changes in the synaptic apparatus and enhanced transmitter production.

Qualitative molecular changes—another alternative of long-term memory

The most sensational—and also most fashionable—theories of memory are those postulating a qualitative change in the RNA and protein molecules within the neuron. These speculations were triggered by the great discovery of our age, the genetic code of the DNA and RNA molecules. The sequence of nucleotides in the deoxyribonucleic acid (DNA) of the chromosomes is a coded message containing a vast amount of information transmitted from generation to generation. Protein synthesis is then started in the cytoplasmic ribosomes according to the information coded in the DNA molecule and transmitted to the cytoplasm by the messenger RNA.

In the wake of this discovery Hydén in Sweden in the 1950's began to study the RNA and DNA of cerebral neurons and their possible role in the retention of memory traces. In his first experiments he tried to establish the relation between the involvement of nerve cells in memory processes and their RNA content. He found that the neuron is the most active RNA producer of the organism. The amount of RNA contained by different neurons of the central nervous system ranges from 20 to 20,000 pg. Those containing amounts close to the upper limit are able to store very much information. If the average information-uptaking capacity of man is 25 bits per second, a person will be able to retain 4 billion bits in 10 years, if we assume 10 hours of information uptake per day. To code this amount of information only two million pairs of nucleotides are needed, which is the number contained by a few neurons. More than 90% of the RNA is found in the cytoplasm of neurons, more precisely in the ribosomes. The nuclei contain very little RNA. As for the amino acid residues, more guanine-cytosine is found in the neurons than adenine-

RNA level in the neuron

207

uracil. Hydén examined the cerebral RNA content of the barracuda, a fish living in the deep waters of the Atlantic Ocean. This fish is known for its remarkable activity and motility. He found a correlation between the motor activity and the cerebral RNA level in these animals (Fig. 58).

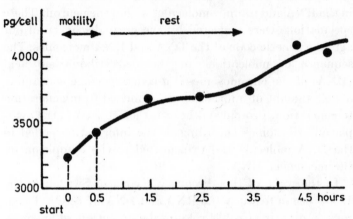

Fig. 58. The RNA level in the barracuda increases much more strongly during motor activity than during rest. Increased activity is thus connected with a higher rate of RNA synthesis (Hydén's observations).

Neuron and glial cell   Hydén also found a connection between nerve cell activity and RNA content from another point of view. He established that the neurons of the spinal cord contain 400 pg RNA per cell at the age of 20, but 700 pg per cell at 40, which again decreases to 400 pg per cell by the age of 80. In further experiments Hydén demonstrated an RNA regulatory system that exists in the neuron and the surrounding glial cells. The latter serve as an energy store for the neuron: a commensurate increase in their RNA content occurs whenever the RNA level of the nerve cell rises.

Proteins   Hydén conducted very interesting experiments in connection with learning and memory. Rats had to balance themselves on a rope tilted at 45° to reach their food on a shelf. In general, this task, which required remarkable skill,

208

took the rats 45 minutes to perform, and took them 4–5 days to learn. The animals were then sacrificed and the RNA content of the medullary Deiters' nuclei determined and compared with the controls. Using a spectacular micro-dissecting technique, Hydén proved that the total amount of RNA as well as the amino acid composition of the nuclear RNA in the vestibular neurons controlling the balancing activity had changed in the experimental animals. The total amount increased, and the proportion of adenine increased while that of uracil decreased (Fig. 59). At the same time the ratio of amino acid residues was unchanged in the *cytoplasmic RNA*. According to Hydén, in the storage mechanisms a major role is played not so much by the quantitative changes (accelerated protein synthesis connected with the increased size of the synapses) as by a specific mode of information storing, similar to the genetic RNA code. There is no evidence, however, to account for the qualitative and quantitative changes occurring in the nucleus, but not in the cytoplasm, in the course of learning. The DNA molecule is an extremely stable component of the cell that will undergo neither quantitative nor qualitative changes in connection with nerve cell function. How can we then explain the change in the composition of RNA for which DNA serves as a template? It has been suggested that the change is due to the electric impulses coming from the membrane. The relation between the periodic digital membrane processes and the intracellular RNA changes is a still unsolved problem of the biological theory of memory retention.

The experiments of McConnell and associates started out in more or less the same direction. They conditioned turbellarian worms. These animals, hardly visible with the naked eye but well observable under the microscope, were stimulated by associated light (conditioned) and electric (unconditioned) stimuli. The conditioned response was swimming. When 100% learning was attained the worms were

Experiments with Planaria

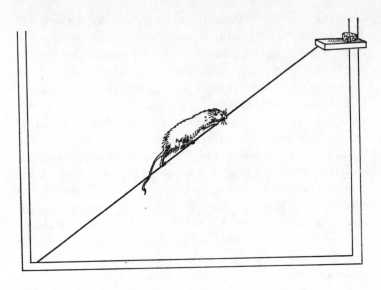

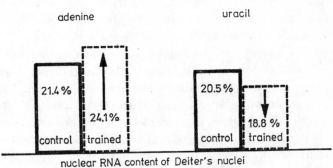

adenine   uracil

21.4%   20.5%

24.1%   18.8%

control trained   control trained

nuclear RNA content of Deiter's nuclei

Fig. 59. Hydén's rats learning to balance. The adenine content increased and the uracil content decreased in the nuclear RNA of the Deiters' nuclei of the trained animals.

cut into two, the head parts were discarded and the tail parts were left to regenerate. (Planarians regenerate very quickly.) To their surprise, the experimenters found that the worms with the new head were capable of the learned response, the same as the original worms before being

210

severed. The information for this response could only have been stored in the neuroblast cells of the tail part.

Other similarly striking experiments were also conducted by the same team. The most exciting of these was the experiment connected with the "cannibalism" of *Planaria*. Conditioned reflexes were established in a group of worms. The animals were killed and their bodies crushed in a mortar, and the cell debris so obtained was fed to untrained worms. The "naive" animals were immediately capable of the reflex responses learned by the worms they had eaten.

The experiments in McConnell's laboratory started an avalanche of experiments which all tried to prove or disprove the feasibility of "memory transfer." The experiments with the cannibal worms were allegedly reproduced by some workers, while others reported negative results.

It has also been claimed that the transfer occurs by means of RNA molecules. To show this experimentally, the worms were kept in a solution containing ribonuclease, the enzyme that breaks down RNA. In these animals the learned response and memory transfer could not be observed. The reverse experiment was also made: RNA was extracted from trained worms and given to the naive ones instead of the whole body extract. A transfer of the learned response was claimed to have occurred in this case.

The sensational experiments on *Planaria* were accepted with mixed feelings. Since the turbellarian worm is a species of simple organization and great regenerating capacity, it was first supposed that the administered "memory code" was somehow integrated into the substance of the nervous system of the animals. However, the more experienced research workers showed scepticism.

Memory transfer in mammals

There soon appeared several papers reporting on transfer phenomena observed in mammals, which immediately led to heated controversy in the international literature. The first reports were published in 1965 by Scandinavian, Czechoslovak, and American workers almost simultaneously. According to the reports, the whole brain or RNA extracts of trained animals stimulated the conditioned reflex activity of untrained ones. We, too, performed experiments along these lines, and although they confirmed the stimulating effect of brain extract on learning, they also proved that this was not due to "memory transfer", but only to the nonspecific stimulating effect of some of the components. Such substances had earlier been extracted from animal organs without any claim being made of having discovered the "memory code"!

"Memory transfer" by chemical means or the solving of the "memory code" thus seems to have been proved illusionary—at least at the present stage of development of molecular biology. The years of great expectations in the 1960's were followed by years of disillusionment and of more sober exploration. It is not impossible that the peptides of brain extracts containing more or less amino acid may play a stimulating role in information retention. Peptides stimulating learning were, in fact, produced by G. Ungar in Houston and by others. But even Ungar would not claim today that, e.g., scotophobin, a peptide of 15 amino acids—a sensational discovery some years ago—contains the "memory code" of the rat's light-avoiding conditioned reflex. Rather, he regards it as a stimulating substance promoting the synaptic transmission of impulses.

The molecular theory of memory is, as can be seen, extremely controversial. Even Hydén's pioneer experiments have not been unequivocally corroborated. The arguments for the closed-circuit hypothesis of short-term memory as well as for the theory of synaptic rearrangement are somewhat more numerous. However, the last word has not been said in this respect either.

Synthesis of theories   Recently there has been a tendency to combine the three best-proved theories of memory (Fig. 60). According to this concept, the *electric*, *synaptic*, and *molecular* processes of memory triggered by repeated external stimuli are

212

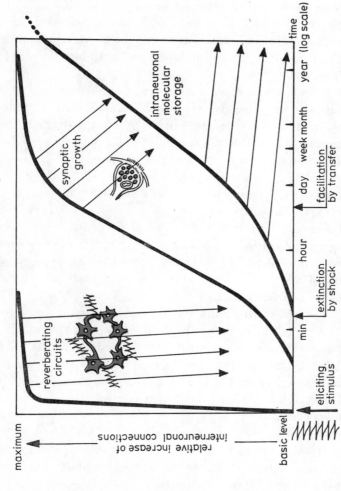

Fig. 60. Scheme of a possible combination of the biological theories of memory. The parallel thin arrows indicate the speed of extinction (forgetting) (after Roberts).

dependent on one another and occur in succession as follows:

1. A series of sensory impulses arranged in a frequency code starts a reverberating activity in a self-stimulating circuit. The reverberating digital signals represent, as an overall effect, information stored in an analog manner. These memory traces are labile and only last for a short time.

2. In the case of very intensive, frequently repeated, or emotionally strongly motivated stimuli, the rhythmic changes in membrane potential—by a hitherto unclarified mechanism—accelerate the intercellular protein synthesis. The reproduction of RNA in the neurons is nonspecifically stimulated, resulting in an increased rate of protein synthesis. This process leads to an increase in the size of the synaptic interface between the cells. From the cybernetic point of view this, too, is an analog process. Information is not carried by a single neuron but by the neuronal network interconnected by the synapses the functional capacity of which has increased. The memory traces thus established are fairly stable.

3. Finally, with impulses of extreme duration or intensity, a qualitative change in the RNA-protein system of the neuron cannot be excluded either. Similarly to the DNA-RNA system of the genetic code, the incoming electric impulses may lead to the formation of a qualitatively different RNA, which would then control the synthesis of a specific protein carrying the memory code.

It will be clear from what has been said above that the storage of memory traces can currently only be explained by a series of inspiring theories.

A uniform system of memory? The possibility of a memory code, similar to the genetic code, has led to speculations among which the most daring even postulate a *uniform* system of memory for the entire

214

living world. No doubt the coding of information passed down from generation to generation has been proved, and the memory of the species is no longer a hypothesis. The same might be said about the memory system of defense mechanisms: the antigen-antibody reaction, i.e., the immune response, is a highly plastic process, one might say a "learned reaction", which often lasts throughout the life of the individual. Confronting these facts with the memory storing processes outlined above, we can appreciate just how attractive such a generalization might appear. Is it not possible that the cerebral mechanisms of memory in the individual, the lasting reactions of immunological "memory", and the genetic memory of the species are merely different aspects of the same biological law? The inventiveness and ingenuity of scientists will no doubt eventually help to find the answer.

Further Readings

ÁDÁM, G.: *Interoception and Behaviour.* Akadémiai Kiadó, Budapest 1967, pp. 1–152.

BUCHHOLTZ, CH.: *Das Lernen bei Tieren: Grundbegriffe der modernen Biologie.* Vol. 11. Gustav Fischer Verlag, Stuttgart 1973, pp. 1–160.

DEUTSCH, J. A.: *The Physiological Basis of Memory.* Academic Press, New York and London 1973, pp. 1–439.

GRAY, J. A.: *Elements of a Two-Process Theory of Learning.* Academic Press, New York 1975, pp. 1–423.

HILGARD, E. E., BOWER, G. H.: *Theories of Learning* (4th ed.). Prentice Hall, Englewood Cliffs 1975.

LURIA, A. R.: *The Neuropsychology of Memory.* V. H. Winston & Sons, Washington, D. C. 1976, pp. 1–372.

McGAUGH, J. L. (ed.): *Psychobiology: Behavior from a Biological Perspective.* Academic Press, New York 1971, pp. 1–366.

MILLER, E. N.: *Selected Papers.* Aldine, Chicago 1971, pp. 1–874.

MILNER, M. P.: *Physiological Psychology.* Holt, Rinehart and Winston, New York 1971, pp. 1–531.

MONNIER, M.: *Functions of the Nervous System.* Vol. 3. *Sensory Functions and Perception.* Elsevier Scientific Publishing Company, Amsterdam 1975, pp. 1–1040.

PAPPAS, G. D., PURPURA, D. P.: *Structure and Function of Synapses.* Raven Press, New York 1972, pp. 1–308.

QUARTON, G. C., MELNECHUK, T., SCHMITT, F. O. (eds.): *The Neurosciences. A study program.* Rockefeller University Press, New York 1967, pp. 1–962.

SCHMITT, F. O. (ed.): *The Neurosciences. Second study program.* Rockefeller University Press, New York 1970, pp. 1–1068.

SCHMITT, F. O., WORDEN, F. G. (eds.): *The Neurosciences. Third study program.* MIT Press, Cambridge, Massachusetts 1974, pp. 1–1107.

SOMJEN, G.: *Sensory Coding in the Mammalian Nervous System.* Appleton-Century-Crofts, New York 1975, pp. 1–386.

Index

Italic numbers refer to pages with figures

219

desynchronization (*see also* alpha blockade) 37, 130, 132
differential inhibition 36
differentiation 188
  method of 18
digestion, control of 125
digital process 24
digital-to-analog conversion 40
direction
  of movement 91
  of moving light 52
  of sounds, perception of 80, 81
discrimination 18
disinhibition 188
distance, visual perception of (*see also* visual perception) 71
DNA 207, 209
Dodt 66
dominators 54, *55*
"down" neurons of the auditory cortex 81
dreams 138
drive 191
dual pathway 118
duplicity theory 53
dynamic stereotypes 181

ear drum (*see also* tympanic membrane) 75
Eccles 205
Economo 136
Edinger–Westphal nucleus 65
EEG waves *129*
  in sleep *138, 141*
  origin of 131
electrical resistance of the skin 39
electric shock 198
electric stimulation 34
electroencephalography 36, *106* 129
  clinical application of 131

electroencephaloscopic screen 134
electromagnetic waves 47, *48*
emotional reactions 154
encoding 25
  in smell perception 100
  in taste perception 100
  of interoceptive impulses 109
encoding system of vision 56
end bulbs *23*, 200, 206
  accelerated protein synthesis in 206
engram 193
epinephrine 123
epiphysis *155*
evoked potentials 37, *38*, 133
  conditioned 198
experience, role of, in perception 45
experimental techniques 17
external inhibition 186, 190
exteroceptors 41, 42
extinction 187
extirpation 33
extracellular fluid 19, *29*
eye
  movements of 65, *66*
    in sleep *138, 139*
  muscles 65, *66*
  optic system 49

facilitation 181
Fechner 42
Fechner's law 43, 92
feedback 126
Forbes 196
forgetting 150
free nerve endings 94
frequency code 30
  for smell 103
  for tastes 103
  in interoceptors 110
frequency, perception of 80

222

medial geniculate body (MGB)
76, 78
medulla 100
   autonomic centers in 125
medulla oblongata *108, 155*
medullary inhibition 128
medullary taste neurons 103
Meissner corpuscles 94
memory 167, 193
   immunological 215
   in old age 197
   long-term 197, 200
   qualitative molecular changes
     in 207
   of species 215
   short-term 196
memory trace 193
memory transfer 211, 212
Merkel corpuscles 84
methods, objective 33
   problem of 32
   psychological 32
microelectrodes 18, 34, 197
micromethods 17
micromorphology 18
micromovements, role of, in
   vision *67*
microscopic anatomy 18
middle ear 75
mitochondrium *202*
modulators 54, *55*
monoaminooxidase (MAO) 139
monocular vision 71
Moruzzi 122, 128, 148
motivation 191
motor neurons of spinal cord
   127
Mountcastle 43, 89, *91*, 96, 99
mouth-tongue projection area
   of the cortex 103
movements of the head, perception of 86
moving light stimulus 61

Müller 32
muscle spindles 84, *85*
myelin sheath 21, *22, 202*

nasal mucous membrane,
   receptor zone of 102
negative induction 190
"negative" learning 187
Negishi 197
neo-Freudian theories 149
nerve cell 21
nerve fiber 21
   insulation of 28
Neumann 26
neuron 21, *23*, 208
noise 26
norepinephrine 139
nucleolus *23*
nucleus *23*
nucleus ventralis posterior (VP)
   of the thalamus 89

objective methods 33
OFF cells 49, *51, 52*, 57, 58,
   61, *63*
old age, memory in 197
Olds *156*
olfactory epithelium 103
ON cells 49, *51, 52*, 57, 58, 61,
   63
"one-way" impulses 91
operant conditioning *175*
operant learning (*see also* instrumental learning) 174
opsin 54
optic nerve 49, *58*
oral cavity, taste buds in 100,
   101
orienting reflex 119
Orne 145
osmoreceptors 42, 109
otoliths 86
output signals 26

15*